ESTATE PLANNING WAR STORIES

View Legal

REFERENCE GUIDE

MATTHEW BURGESS

National Library of Australia Cataloguing-in-Publication entry

Creator:	Burgess, Matthew, author.
Title:	Estate planning war stories: reference guide / Matthew Burgess; book designed by Dedicated Book Services.
ISBN:	978-1-925406-36-8 (paperback)
ISBN:	978-1-925406-37-5 (ebook : Kindle)
ISBN:	978-1-925406-38-2 (ebook : epub)
Subjects:	Burgess, Matthew.
	Estate planning—Australia—Case studies.
	Trusts and trustees—Australia—Case studies.
	Future interests—Australia—Case studies.
	Probate law and practice—Australia—Case studies.
	Estates (Law)—Australia—Case studies

Other Creators/Contributors: Dedicated Book Services, book designer.

Dewey Number: 332.024016

Estate Planning War Stories – Reference Guide

Published by D & M Fancy Pastry in 2017

Typefaces: ElectraLTStd

Contents

Foreword

Matthew Burgess, Patrick Ellwood and Tara Lucke are co founders, with Naomi Arnold, of View Legal.

Having previously founded Australia's first virtual law firm as a wholly owned subsidiary of one of the country's leading independent law firms, View Legal is results focused and passionate about delivering new solutions in a way that aligns with their 'SPS' – service and price satisfaction guarantee.

As author of technical legal books, Matthew is widely recognised as constantly creating innovative strategies for the growth, management and protection of wealth.

Published legal books include:

(1) The Nine Steps to a Complete Estate Plan
(2) The Seven Foundations of Business Succession
(3) Five Essential Estate Planning Articles
(4) The Seven Key Aspects of Testamentary Trusts
(5) Inside Stories – the complete collection of blog posts
(6) The Five Foundations of SMSFs
(7) Six Foundations of the Taxation of Trusts
(8) Six Essential Structuring Articles
(9) The Nine Foundations of Asset Protection
(10) 40 Forms of Trusts – Workbook

Introduction

Story telling is often seen as the cornerstone of explaining any principle. Certainly my experience in the estate planning area is that there are few approaches as memorable as learning based on 'war stories'.

This workbook collects client based and court decision scenarios that explain 10 key estate planning principles.

The 10 key principles are:

(1) Don't become a war story
(2) It's the 'vibe'
(3) Let's kill all the lawyers
(4) Estate planning is more than a will
(5) Don't get stuck in the middle
(6) Murphy's Law
(7) Iterate & update
(8) Just do it
(9) No estate plan, means you have an estate plan
(10) It depends

In relation to the stories shared that are not reported court decisions, it is critical to note that they are all based, or in some instances inspired, by true stories.

One of the fundamental reasons why I have been fortunate enough to assist so many successful people is that I maintain complete confidentiality and respect for privacy in relation to their affairs.

For example, the statement that I have assisted a significant number of the BRW top 200 'Rich List' does not provide a great deal of insight into whom I have actually worked with over the years - for three main reasons:

a   while many have been assisted, there is a far greater percentage that I have not assisted b   a cursory review of the list shows that it is constantly evolving; indeed only 18 people have made every list since it started in 1984

c   perhaps most interestingly, many of my clients are extremely disciplined about financial privacy, and therefore, despite the investigative reporting skills of the compilers of 'rich lists', these individuals are not profiled at all, even though, in some instances, they would be in the top 10% of the lists.

It is important to note that, in relation to all of the case study examples provided, critical factual aspects have been changed, so as to protect the identity of the people involved; this does not affect the fundamental principle.

Examples of the changes are:

a   gender of the person
b   industry involved
c   quantum of wealth
d   references to years, timeframes etc

Many of these stories have formed the basis of seminar programs I have presented over the years and all are derived from actual client situations.

This said, all stories ultimately avoid the mistake I made some years ago, as explained in the 'Last Flight to Fiji' story. In other words, key factual changes are made to every story to ensure any similarity to actual people or situations is merely coincidental.

Each of the 10 chapters explains a discrete or standalone principle.

There is one other 'disclaimer', one story from each chapter in this book is replicated from material originally published in my business book 'The Dream Enabler'. That book consolidates my learnings from two decades of assisting some of Australia's most successful people into nine key attributes. A part of each principle explored in that book is then also highlighted via story telling.

The Dream Enabler book is written primarily for clients. This book is designed for advisers, hence the republication of a number of stories from The Dream Enabler.

First Principle

DON'T BECOME A WAR STORY

“The colossal misunderstanding of our time is the assumption that insight will work with people who are unmotivated to change. Communication does not depend on syntax, or eloquence, or rhetoric, or articulation but on the emotional context in which the message is being heard. People can only hear you when they are moving toward you, and they are not likely to when your words are pursuing them. ”

— *Edwin Friedman*

Back of the envelope

Client Scenario

PASSION IS OFTEN seen as the 'secret ingredient' that is the difference between success and failure.

The age old saying that *'if you can find a job that you love, you will never work a day in your life'*, is often quoted by ultra successful people.

The extent of the passion that drives many successful people is sometimes difficult to comprehend unless it is experienced firsthand.

In the early 2000s, I was fortunate enough to work for a tourism operator named Ross, who had spent what ended up being the last 20 years of his career developing an extraordinary island eco tourism resort.

At various times, almost singlehandedly, he battled with governments of each persuasion and at local, state and federal levels.

There were then the battles with impatient investors, family members that had different visions to his and financiers that had grown tired of, what they saw as, never ending delays.

The project in many respects was all-consuming and, shortly before the resort was finally ready to open, the headaches that Ross had been experiencing for some months became so unbearable that he decided to go to his GP.

He completed the initial course of medication for what were thought to be severe migraines, but after two more weeks of increasing pain he went back to his GP who referred him for specialist help.

Ross was sent to hospital for brain scans, at which point he was told that a brain tumour as big as a tennis ball had been discovered just behind his left eye.

Further tests and surgery were deemed useless. Ross had, at best, four weeks to live.

While a cocktail of drugs would at least help manage the pain, they would also severely diminish his capacity, and with the project still at least 12 weeks from completion, he realised that he must assign a priority to every activity, knowing that whatever was not near the top of the list would simply never be done.

He also knew that anything not addressed in the first couple of weeks following the diagnosis was also highly unlikely to be done, as the medication required to numb his pain would increase to levels that would make even getting out of bed virtually impossible.

Perhaps understandably, even for someone with such enormous passion for his life's work, Ross essentially let go of the remaining steps of the project. Fortunately, he had surrounded himself with a management team and family members who understood his vision He called a series of meetings in the 48 hours following the initial diagnosis but that was all the time he was willing to invest.

The priority list, as far as Ross was concerned, had been narrowed down to simply one item – to spend time with his family and friends – and over the next 10 days, as his health deteriorated even more rapidly than had been initially expected, that is exactly what he did.

Long days and even longer nights were filled with meals, stories, laughter and tears – all shared with those nearest to him.

Within two weeks of the initial diagnosis, Ross was re-admitted to hospital and would not leave until his death.

At some point, around 36 hours before he passed away, at a time when the painkillers were at a level that left him barely conscious, a family friend asked Ross whether his executors knew where his will was stored.

For the past two weeks, his passion had dissipated, hour by hour until it appeared non-existent. Now, almost instantaneously, it returned.

No, the executors of Ross' will did not know where the last will was because there was no last will. On two or three occasions over the years, Ross had started estate-planning exercises only to give them up as being useless because so many things were likely to change before he passed away.

Now, with nothing likely to change, he faced the serious prospect of his life's work unravelling with a suite of legal fees and government rules. There would be family members left guessing, at best, and fighting bitterly, at worst, about what his intentions might be.

Using the back of an envelope retrieved from a nearby rubbish bin by his friend, and the pen normally attached to the clipboard at the end of his hospital bed, Ross sketched out the vision for his estate plan and asked his friend to arrange for his accountant to draft the necessary documents, so that he could review and sign them the following day.

The instructions on the back of the envelope were extraordinarily detailed (despite being set out on such a small piece of paper) and made logical sense, the task that I had been given, via Ross' accountant, was at best extremely difficult, and more realistically, completely impossible.

We put together base documentation and had it ready for review by the next morning as requested, but without an in-depth meeting with Ross and his accountant, it was likely that what we had produced would in fact be worse than not having any will at all.

At 9am the next morning, the accountant and I arrived at the hospital ward, and waited while the doctor on duty confirmed that Ross could in fact see visitors.

Ross' wife and one of his sons explained to us that he was exceptionally weak, and while his mental capabilities seemed sound, the drugs had had such a severe impact that we should expect only a very short and extremely high level discussion.

When the doctor motioned to us to enter the room, his only comment was that, if possible, we should arrange to have all documentation signed immediately; in his opinion, Ross had only about 24 hours to live.

As we entered the room, with Ross' wife close behind, we were immediately struck by the passion and energy in his voice. Physically, he was as bad, possibly worse, than we expected, but his vocal demeanour was in complete contrast.

For the next hour we vigorously debated every aspect of his vision, referring to a photocopy of his envelope summary that I had blown up onto an A3 size piece of paper.

The accountant and I left the room positive that the series of instructions we had been given captured all of his vision. I was thinking that if that if Ross could perform like that when he was near death, he must have been an extraordinary operator in full flight.

His wife must have read my mind. She had maintained complete composure throughout the hour long meeting, but now had trouble controlling her voice as tears streamed down her cheeks. 'It was as if nothing was wrong with him at all', she repeated over and over again, as, nearly collapsing, she was helped by her son to a nearby chair.

Four hours later, the accountant and I were back in the same hospital room with Ross.

Already physically depleted, his verbal and mental capacities were now rapidly fading.

The energy, passion and strength that had so impressed us only a few hours earlier had almost completely disappeared.

In a meeting that lasted less than 10 minutes, we were barely able to walk through the headline components of the documentation before Ross began slipping in and out of consciousness.

While we managed to get all documentation signed, our strong sense on leaving the room was that we were most likely to be the last people to speak with him, and we were proved correct. Two hours later, Ross died.

The passion with which he had been able to confirm his vision for his estate plan was at the time, and remains to this day, truly inspirational.

Court Decision

Peter Wright was Lang Hancock's business partner in iron ore operations in Western Australia.

Wright, who had been diagnosed with stomach cancer in late 2011, died aged 74 on April 26, 2012.

Before his death in 2007, he set up a trust named the Olivia Trust No 2 (which contained commercial property and $20,000 cash).

The trust was to be gifted, on highly conditional terms, $3 million (through five payments).

A clause in the will specified that the payments were in support of Olivia and they represented 'adequate and proper maintenance, support, education and advancement in the life of Olivia Mead'.

There were a number of conditions which allowed the trustee to declare a beneficiary to be an excluded beneficiary on events such as:

(1) Becoming an alcoholic;
(2) Drug Conviction or conviction for association with drugs;
(3) In opinion of the trustee, suspected association with illegal drugs;
(4) In opinion of the trustee, has become a drug addict;
(5) A member of a religious body other than 'Roman Catholic, Anglican, Presbyterian, Baptist, Uniting or other similar traditional faiths';
(6) Convicted of a felony.

Olivia challenged the estate and brought a family provision claim. She expressed desires for:

a $1.2 million (US) Kuhn-Bosendorfer piano;
b a $250,000 Ritter Royal Flora Aurum bass guitar (the world's most expensive – the 'diamond crusted guitar');
c Jimmy Choo shoes, Tiffany sunglasses;
d $100,000 wedding;
e $2.5 million home; and
f a rabbit, a ferret, a dog, an axolotl.

The estate was estimated to be valued at $1.5 billion.

Olivia had no idea the trust actually existed at the time of making her initial challenge.

The Judge's opening statement was: 'The deceased's estate is colossal. By reference to the statement of assets and liabilities attached to the affidavit sworn by the first defendant the value of each of the second and third defendant's entitlements is in the order of $400 million.'

The main issues in the case were:

(1) Was Olivia adequately provided for? Including proper maintenance, support, education or advancement in her lifetime; and

(2) If no, then the court has discretion to make provision taking into account the facts at the time of the order.

In relation to the first question, that is -was she adequately provided for, ultimately the court thought that she was not adequately provided for. The Judge said that the starting point was considering the size of the estate.

The court held that the whole trust structure that had been set up was 'unwieldy' and unworkable. In particular it was held that the solicitor trustee, who had never met Olivia, would never be able to understand the needs of a 19 year old girl.

Adequate in the relevant Act as 'sufficiency' but the Judge went further to say that there was no reason why the court can't consider 'suitable' as defined in the Macquarie dictionary.

The discretion of the court is 'unfettered' and it must be exercised in a judicial manner, but there is nothing in the Act which assumes the award should be no more than adequate provision.

The Judge indicated it was a judicial balancing of the:

a Size of the estate;
b Needs of the plaintiff; and
c Interests of other parties.

It was held that the size of the estate was so large that the 'value [is] irrelevant in determining the outcome'.

The Judge indicated that because of the size of the estate, no other party would be prejudiced by any award made, regardless of how large the award was.

In the circumstance the decision handed down was as follows:

(1) $25 million (this amount was considered for the estate to be a 'rounding error').

(2)   The biggest influencing factor was the size of the estate.

(3)   The award was said to make no difference to the other beneficiaries (who were thought to be receiving at least $400 million each).

(4)   The decision specifically commented that it was not about 'fairness' or compensation.

The court ultimately applied a 'wise and just willmaker approach'. The relevant comments in this regard were as follows:

> This (concept) conjures up the rather archaic image of a grey haired gentleman in a smoking jacket, pipe in mouth, sitting at a leather top desk, fountain pen in hand, attempting to balance the interests of his wife and children. With that image in mind the internal dialogue might go something like this:
>
> I am a fabulously wealthy man. I am able to provide for my wife, my children and others to such an extent that all will be well provided for without any of the others suffering. My two daughters Leonie and Alexandra have proved themselves loyal and have run the Voyager Estate business extremely well. They have supported me in every possible way. They deserve the lion's share of my estate and they will have it. My son Myles is a successful musician who has forged his own career without much help from me. I should provide for him, conscious of the knowledge he has not been involved in the family business and will always be in a position to provide for himself.
>
> That leaves my daughter Olivia. At her age she has no real idea of what she wants to do - she might get married and have

four children. She might become an arts administrator when she finishes university or she may change her mind. She should have complete financial security so that she can pursue whatever interests she wishes into the future. She is young but she is level headed and with sound advice she can doubtless invest anything I leave to her to provide for her long term benefit. I can afford to spoil her and there is no reason why I should not do so.

The 'Community expectations' test was also applied and it was held that 'most people would expect the plaintiff to be more than adequately provided for'. This meant specifically that the:

a Judge indicated $25 million would not fall outside the scope of the community's expectations;

b community expectations test 'cuts both words'. In other words, it is reasonable for a willmaker to exclude a long estranged child (20+ years) – see the case of (Burke v Burke [2015] NSWCA 195.

Second Principle

IT'S THE VIBE

> **" A quitter never wins and a winner never quits. "**
>
> — *Napoleon Hill*

The great, great, great nephews

Client Scenario

U NDERSTANDING THE DISTINCTION between dogged persistence that delivers success from the jaws of failure and blind, but ultimately totally misplaced, faith leading to irreversible disaster is often the single biggest factor that sets the truly wealthy apart.

For over a generation, David, a particularly successful retail business operator had owned a significant parcel of land on the coastline in northern New South Wales.

Within the space of about 10 years, the land had been effectively surrounded by developments. A resort had been built on land immediately to the north, unit blocks on the land to the south and to the west only a 2-lane highway separated his land from a commercial estate.

David, despite countless offers, remained steadfast in his vision that his parcel of land would remain largely undeveloped, but for an eco style resort, reserved solely for school excursion visits.

By virtually any test, the vision was impressive.

The only real difficulty was a lack of liquid funds needed to build the basic infrastructure and to maintain the asset, including expenses such as local council rates and state government land tax charges.

By the early 1990s, having held the property for over 30 years, David, now into his late 80s, found the holding costs were becoming prohibitive. He spent most of his time lobbying both state and local government to fund the eco development and waive all government charges.

His vision had remained essentially unchanged for over a decade and through numerous changes of government, the negotiations with various bureaucrats and department representatives had followed a very similar pattern:

a   David would list his various funding demands
b   the relevant government officials would push back for some liquid financial contribution from David
c   David would then invariably discontinue discussions on the basis that his undertaking to ensure that the property would be available for school children to visit 'indefinitely' was more than enough of a contribution.

Throughout this period, countless developers brought proposals to David. While many proposed a straight sale of the bulk of the property in return for a share of any development profits, some proposals would have enabled the funding of virtually all of David's vision with a relatively small proportion of the total landholding needing to be sold.

One proposal in particular would have involved a boutique development of only ten townhouses on one corner of the property. The eco retreat would be built at the same time as the townhouse development, and sufficient funds would have been provided upfront to establish a trust fund that, in perpetuity, would have delivered sufficient interest to cover all government charges, without any concessions.

As he had done throughout his business career, David remained unmoved by all of these offers. The only approach that aligned with his vision involved the entire parcel remaining dedicated to his eco resort for school children. The need for ongoing funds would, in his view, be minimal, as long as the various levels of government were committed to the vision.

As David's health deteriorated over the last five years of his life, the level of interest from both government and property developers in the know began to dwindle. His demands had remained virtually unchanged for close to 15 years and he began to turn his attention to others whom he felt he could trust to deliver his vision, once the government finally bowed to his demands.

The three main actors in what turned out to be the last 12 months of David's life were:

a   his lawyer, who was based over two hours' drive from the property where David continued to live until the time of his death

b   David's two great, great, great nephews; one had never met David and the other had met him only twice

c   David's personal carers, both of whom lived with him on the property, and were in their late 60s, having retired from employment.

In the last nine months of David's life, he made eleven wills.

In the last three months of his life, he made seven wills.

His final will gave the parcel of land to his personal carers, and on discovering this, the two great, great, great nephews challenged its legitimacy, arguing that David must have lacked the capacity to understand what he was doing.

There was no doubt that the great, great, great nephews had a potential case. One of the listed causes of death was dementia and while the medical specialists had been unable to determine how long David had been suffering from the condition, clearly it had been for some years.

Perhaps coincidentally, while the great, great, great nephews were challenging the last will, they were just as robustly arguing the validity of the second last will, written only a few days earlier.

Under the terms of the second last will, the two great, great, great nephews had been named as executors of the estate and inheritors of the property – entitled to take the land in equal shares.

Because the last will had been prepared only a few days after the previous one, it meant that virtually all the arguments that the great, great, great nephews raised in questioning David's mental capacity when he signed his last will were in fact likely to be just as compelling evidence for the invalidity of the second last will, for exactly the same reasons.

Somewhat predictably, the third last will, done some weeks before the second last will, had given David's estate to his personal carers, and appointed them the executors.

In contrast, the fourth last will again saw the great, great, great nephews being nominated as the executors and beneficiaries.

This pattern continued on a 'turn and turnabout' basis over countless wills.

The lawyer had file notes recording the creation of each will. He would receive a phone call from David asking for changes to be made to his will. The changes would be made, the solicitor would drive over two hours to the beach shack where David lived, have the document signed, then drive a further two hours back to his office.

On each occasion, the lawyer charged David a fee of $120. By his own admission, this would have barely covered his petrol expenses.

Again perhaps coincidentally, the co executor of every one of the last dozen or so wills was the same lawyer. In the first year after David's death, the legal fees in relation to the administration of the estate alone were more than the fees the lawyer had generated from all other clients in the previous four years of his practice.

After advice from two separate law firms and almost two years of litigation, the personal carers were struggling to maintain their energy levels. It was at this time that they approached our firm.

Throughout the same period, the great, great, great nephews had used a law firm that operated on a 'no fees unless we win' basis.

In contrast, our firm's fees were paid without fail within a 14-day period at the end of each month. How the personal carers achieved this, given that they continued to live in the beach shack with their only source of income being a government pension, was something that, perhaps naïvely, I did not understand for some years after the case was eventually settled.

In this type of litigation, the lawyers for both parties will effectively 'grandstand' their client's position right up to the steps of the courtroom on the first scheduled day of the hearing. Invariably at that point, there is a real incentive for all parties to settle rather than go through the lottery of a trial.

Regardless of how strong you think your case might be, the reality is that your prospect of success can never be more than 70%, given the number of variables at play inside a courtroom and the subjective opinions of the judge.

Conversely, no matter how weak your case might be, you always have about a 30% chance of winning.

Here, the win-loss prospects were more likely 50-50, given that all of the evidence gathered by both parties 'proving' the invalidity of the will that gave the land to the other side was just as likely to be used against them, because the last few wills were done within a few months of each other.

Although the case did reach the courtroom, it was adjourned after 30 minutes and, by the end of what should have been the first day of the trial, a settlement had been struck.

David's very last will was agreed by the parties to be his true and final intention.

The great, great, great nephews' support for this conclusion was guaranteed on the undertaking that they would receive a significant 7-figure payment.

Within four months of the settlement, Harvey one of the property developers who had many years earlier put arguably the least most attractive proposal to David had acquired the property from the personal carers.

Within five years of the date of settlement, the entire parcel of land had been fully developed with a series of unit blocks, a retail precinct, including a fuel station, and two office blocks.

The only area of the entire parcel of land that was remotely likely to be of interest to school age children was the obligatory swing set and slippery dip that was shaded in the afternoon by one of the office blocks that caught the setting sun.

The way in which our firm's legal fees had been paid throughout the litigation period, and indeed, the way the pensioners had met all of their financial obligations was disclosed to me some years later.

It was revealed that, within days of David's death, the personal carers had been approached by Harvey and had signed both a confidentiality agreement and a call option deed.

The confidentiality agreement prohibited them talking to anyone, including their lawyers, about the nature of the deal they had struck with Harvey.

The call option deed gave Harvey the right to acquire the parcel of land, as long as the personal carers won the litigation (which obviously they ultimately did).

The price for the granting of the option was the total of all legal fees incurred by the personal carers as well as the payment of any settlement amount to the great, great, great nephews.

The strike price under the option was then a further additional amount by way of actual purchase price.

The total amount paid by Harvey in relation to the three components (legal fees, settlement payment and purchase price), although it ran to many millions of dollars, ultimately proved to be less than $1/8^{th}$ of the total value of the landholding, and by some accounts, actually proved to be less than $1/30^{th}$ of the total profit from the development.

The steadfast persistence of David meant that not only did his vision never materialise, but a group of lawyers and a property developer made astronomical profits.

Court Decision

The widely publicised High Court judgment of Stanford v Stanford (2012) HCA 52 from the end of 2012 highlights the Family Courts' powers to potentially displace the distribution of assets under an estate plan.

The brief facts were that Mr and Mrs Stanford had no children together, although both had children from previous relationships. The Stanford's had both crafted their estate plans to provide for their respective children, without making provision for each other, other than a life tenancy in the family home.

The house was owned solely in the name of Mr Stanford (he had bought it before the marriage), although it had been lived in by the couple for over 40 years.

Critically, Mrs Stanford appointed her children, not Mr Stanford, under her guardian and attorney documents.

Due to ill health and mental incapacity, Mrs Stanford was moved into residential care. Despite no suggestion that the couple were anything other than happily married, on her mother's incapacity Mrs Stanford's daughter initiated proceedings in the Family Court (as Mrs Stanford's legal guardian).

The orders requested were for equal division of the marital property (the main asset was the family home) between Mr and Mrs Stanford.

The initial Judge ordered that Mr Stanford pay a fixed sum of approximately half the value of the marital property to Mrs Stanford, which payment would have effectively passed directly to her guardians.

To fund the payment the family home would have needed to be sold, forcing Mr Stanford to leave the house.

Mr Stanford appealed the decision, however Mrs Stanford passed away before judgment was delivered by the Court of Appeal. The Court of Appeal ultimately decided that Mrs Stanford's legal personal representatives should receive the fixed sum upon the death of Mr Stanford.

This decision effectively altered the distribution of Mr Stanford's estate (which Mrs Stanford had agreed with while she had capacity) under his will as the house (following his wife's death) would have otherwise passed to his children.

The decision of the Court of Appeal was ultimately set aside on appeal to the High Court, on the basis that the order was not just and equitable. However, importantly, the High Court confirmed that the death of a party to a marriage 'does not transform the nature of the claim (for example, into a claim by the beneficiaries of the wife's estate)'.

In other words, the right of a guardian or attorney to commence property settlement proceedings was effectively confirmed, even where (as here) they would have no entitlement to challenge the estate of their step father.

The decision highlights the risks that in some cases, particularly in relation to blended families, estate distributions may be fundamentally altered by way of 'pre-emptive' proceedings through the family law court.

Arguably, particularly given the decision in the courts below the High Court, the final decision is an example of the legal principle first applied in the Australian documentary movie 'The Castle' (lawyers view the movie as a documentary, most non-lawyers will remember the movie as an iconic comedy).

In contrast to the above decision, the case of McKenzie & McKenzie [2013] FCCA 1013 is also interesting.

A summary of the facts is as follows:

(1)   the wife separated from the husband, and around six months later, there was evidence to suggest that she began preparing documentation to apply for a divorce;

(2)   around nine months after the initial separation, the wife underwent surgery that ultimately resulted in her losing capacity;

(3)   following the loss of capacity, the wife's mother was appointed her legal guardian

(4)   via her role as legal guardian, the wife's mother formally finalised an application for divorce;

(5)   the court allowed the divorce proceedings to proceed on the application of the mother on the basis that the relationship between her daughter and former son-in-law had broken down irretrievably before the loss of capacity; and

(6)   the fact that the daughter had not been separated from the husband for 12 months (which is normally required) before she lost capacity was not held to be relevant in the circumstances. Again, arguably 'the vibe' applied to help get to the 'appropriate' answer.

Third Principle

LET'S KILL ALL
THE LAWYERS

"If you don't know where you are going you might end up someplace else.
— *Yogi Berra*

Life planning

Client Scenario

T O EMBARK ON an estate planning exercise is to gain, inevitably a deep insight into someone's true purpose.

People going through the process reflect on what they have achieved so far; they also express the goals and objectives they wish to see future generations aspire to. This stimulates conversations and ideas that are not normally given much airtime.

Views on death, for example, are as diverse as the people who hold them.

An example at one end of the spectrum is that of a famous sport star, whose only substantial direction under his estate plan was (and this is a partial paraphrase) "As long as you play Elvis at the wake, I could not care less what you do with the rest of it".

At the other end was a client with one of the largest jewellery collections in the southern hemisphere. As well as setting up a special purpose trust for one particular ring (admittedly, it had a 7-digit dollar value), she developed a complex formula to determine which of her nieces would be entitled to particular items in the collection.

The formula was reapplied on a yearly basis and all estate planning documentation was updated in accordance with the results, which were largely derived by counting the number of visits, phone calls and direct interactions that the nieces had with their aunt. None of them was aware of the impact that their level of contact was to have on their ultimate inheritance entitlements.

When guiding people through estate planning, one of the most important attributes is the ability to remain impartial and objective.

Everyone's perspective is obviously a result of accumulated life experience. For an outsider who has very little real knowledge of the life journey someone has taken, it is important to try to defer any form of judgement.

From time to time, however, certain situations or requests demand that a stand be taken and, late one Friday evening in 2003, there was such an time.

A request for a meeting at 6.30pm on a Friday was of itself not particularly unusual. Extremely successful people often have narrow windows in which to commit to 'non productive' activities, and for most people, rightly or wrongly, reviewing their estate planning arrangements certainly falls into that category.

I knew about the business success of this client – Bryan was a property developer – it was however the first time I had met him, and his CFO. There were certain complications with his arrangements that seemed to increase as the meeting went on.

For the first hour, the focus was on a web of trusts, companies and partnerships that had evolved over a 30-year career.

Many were dormant or of no particular value because the assets were offset by near equivalent liabilities, but just as many had significant asset holdings.

Some of these valuable assets were held in conjunction with third parties, but the legal relationship with those third parties was based on nothing more than a handshake.

Even where third parties were not involved, the legal and accounting information in relation to each entity was at best scant, and in many instances, simply non-existent.

Despite this, Bryan undoubtedly satisfied most accepted definitions of a 'high net wealth individual', and 90 minutes into the meeting, it became clear that the work required to achieve his objectives would require a significant investment in legal spend and a concerted effort by him, his CFO and external accountants.

Any expenses incurred at this juncture would be only a fraction of the likely costs should Bryan pass away before implementing the necessary steps.

Despite having only scratched the surface of the structural and financial issues that would need to be resolved, the CFO certainly captured my full attention when, with hushed voice, he asked Bryan to move onto the 'more complex' aspect of the meeting, meaning his personal affairs.

Bryan then explained his family tree, which, at least initially, did not seem unduly complex.

He had been married twice.

The first marriage had lasted over 20 years and there were two children from the relationship.

Bryan still maintained strong ties with both children; the son was doing an apprenticeship in his father's business.

There was virtually no relationship between Bryan and his first wife; she had 'completely cleaned me out' following the divorce. The fact that the second wife had been already three months pregnant with their only child before Bryan had officially separated from his first wife would not have helped their relationship. Equally unhelpful was the fact that the second wife was younger than Bryan's daughter from the first marriage.

As Bryan explained it, the relationship with his second wife was strong. He had asked for a 'prenup' (or binding financial agreement) about three or four years before this meeting; this had been received very poorly by the wife because, as the CFO commented, she felt that she had been a significant part of the extraordinary financial success that Bryan had enjoyed since being 'cleaned out' under the property settlement with his first wife.

Even though the son from the second marriage was not yet a teenager, Bryan felt the boy was already demonstrating skills that suggested he could one day take over the management of the business; he certainly showed more promise in this regard than the adult son from the first marriage.

There was no doubt that the personal factual matrix was at least as complex as were the business structures. I had seen far more complex scenarios, however, and had always been able to develop a workable pathway. I immediately set out a number of innovative and practical ideas on how best to address the complexities that had been raised.

The combined effect of a long week and the fact that I had been drawing a number of diagrams on the whiteboard somehow made me miss Bryan's increasing agitation. I had not allowed him to finish the summary of his personal situation. Eventually, my barrage of ideas was stopped quite bluntly by the CFO: "Matthew, we haven't got to the complex part yet!".

As I slowly sank into my chair, Bryan's dark brown eyes locked with mine and held the stare for what seemed like a full minute.

"Two years ago, I started a relatively regular relationship with a prostitute", Bryan announced. The silence that followed seemed to last an unnaturally long time, and the tension in the room was heightened by a long draw on the unfiltered cigarette that seemed to be permanently in the corner of Bryan's mouth.

Having learned my lesson about jumping in too early with feedback, I let him continue.

"About six months into the relationship, she claimed that she was pregnant with my child and since her daughter was born, about 12 months ago, she has been blackmailing me to the tune of $5,000 a month.

Just recently, she said that the amount needed to be nearer to $10,000 and she wants a guarantee that she will receive at least a house and an additional lump sum payment on my death.

Unless I comply, she intends telling my wife about the daughter, but conveniently, she refuses to allow a paternity test.

I am relaxed about providing for the daughter during my lifetime, regardless of the paternity issue; I just see that as a cost of doing business, so as to speak.

What I need you to do is develop a mechanism, in my estate plan, to force the issue of the paternity test. I will only continue support for the daughter after my death if it is actually proved that I am the father".

By this stage, the air in the room was becoming increasingly heavy with smoke – I had forgotten that the air conditioning automatically shut down at 8pm. For another 20 minutes, we explored the various ways in which Bryan's objectives could be achieved. On four or five occasions, however, I had stated that unless specific steps were taken to provide for the mother, then all of my suggestions were at serious risk of failure.

Each time this point was raised, Bryan simply responded, "We will deal with that at the end of the meeting".

By just before 9pm, we seemed to have dealt with all relevant issues and complications and the CFO announced that from his perspective everything had been discussed satisfactorily. As he stood to excuse himself, I reminded him that there remained one last issue: how to best provide for the mother of the young daughter. Before the CFO had a chance to respond, Bryan interjected, "We won't need him for that part of the meeting".

Having ushered the CFO across the now pitch black reception area to the lift well, my mind refocused on what was likely to be the most complex aspect of a very complex situation. Little did I realise how simple the solution devised by Bryan would be and how little work would be required from me on any aspect of his arrangements.

As I shut the meeting room door, the first thing I noticed, even before the fact that yet another unfiltered cigarette had been lit up, was that a black gym bag, probably big enough to hold two adult sized basketballs, was on the mahogany table.

"Do you have a strong room here?" Bryan asked me.

"Of course".

"Your instructions in relation to the outstanding aspect of my estate plan, then, are as follows. First, as soon as you are notified of my death, you will arrange for this gym bag to be called out of secure storage. On receipt, you will open the bag and remove the envelope that you find inside. Inside that envelope is a phone number. You will phone that number.

You will give my name to whoever answers the call, and confirm that you are my lawyer and that I have died.

You will then follow that person's directions to ensure the secure delivery of the gym bag.

Adopting this approach will ensure that there is no need for me to make any provision whatsoever for this woman.

And, in case you need to know, other than the envelope with the mobile phone number, the bag contains $150,000 in cash – $30,000 for you and the balance for the person who collects the bag. Given that you will only spend 10 minutes doing your job, that's an hourly rate of $180,000 for your efforts".

I was totally silent. Not because I was trying to create tension, but because I was completely shocked by what I had just heard. Eventually, I said something like, "I'm not entirely sure what movies you watch, but I assume what you have just explained to me is some sort of joke. Not only will this bag be going nowhere near our secure storage facility, you will never contact our firm again. You can find your own way out of the building this evening".

Bryan's purpose and vision in virtually every aspect of his life were extraordinary.

Unfortunately, in the one area where it arguably mattered most, his purpose fell well short.

Court Decision

Arguably, the most significant cause of the lack of confidence in trusts is the High Court decision of Kennon v Spry [2008] HCA 56, on the basis that it appeared to alter the longstanding principles relating to the asset protection advantages of trusts in the context of a marriage breakdown.

Briefly the situation in this case was as follows.

In 1968, the husband settled a discretionary trust named the ICF Spry Trust, of which he was both the trustee and settlor. The eligible beneficiaries consisted of the 'standard' range of beneficiaries typically found in a discretionary trust, including the husband, any spouse of the husband, the husband's issue, his siblings, their spouses and their issue, and charitable beneficiaries.

In 1978, the husband and the wife married and they subsequently had four daughters.

In 1983, the husband varied the trust deed by excluding himself as a beneficiary and appointing the wife as trustee on his death or resignation. As a result, the husband ceased to be a potential beneficiary. It was understood that this variation was done predominately for land tax purposes.

In December 1998, at a time when the wife argued the relationship was starting to strain, the husband executed a further deed of variation which excluded the wife as a capital beneficiary.

During the course of 2002, the husband established a discretionary trust for each of the four daughters of the marriage, of which he was the initial trustee and was later the joint trustee with a Mr Edwin Philip Kennon.

As trustee of the ICF Spry Trust, the husband then distributed the capital and income of that trust equally between the four children's trusts.

Dr Spry did that effectively, in the court's view, as a way to mean that not only did he not have the assets, so that he could be forced into giving them up to his wife, it also meant that his wife didn't have them either.

Essentially it was his way of saying to the family court 'catch me if you can'.

Following the couple's separation and subsequent divorce, the wife sought orders from the court setting aside the distributions from the ICF Spry Trust to the children's trusts, arguing that the pool of assets for distribution should include the ICF Spry Trust's assets and the income distributed to the children's trusts.

The primary question before the court was whether the pool of assets for distribution on the property settlement should comprise the assets of the ICF Spry trust.

The wife argued that the pool should include the assets in the children's trusts, while the husband alleged that neither the ICF Spry Trust, nor any of the children's trusts, could be considered property or indeed even a financial resource of the parties to the marriage.

The trial judge made orders to set aside the 1998 and 2002 instruments and ordered that the assets of the ICF Spry Trust be included in the pool of assets for division between the parties.

On appeal (ultimately) to the High Court, the majority held (among other things) that the husband's legal ownership of the assets as sole trustee, combined with the wife's interest as a beneficiary of the trust, were a proper basis for the assets of the ICF Spry Trust to be treated as the property of the parties.

This meant the court could, and indeed did, allocate all of the assets of the trust to the wife.

Certainly, immediately following Spry, for an extended period, the usefulness of trusts was under the spotlight and there was significant nervousness about how robust they actually were going to be.

The reality has been that this conclusion has been tempered by the fact that Spry is a somewhat of an outlier decision and actually driven a lot by the factual scenario, which is a relatively strange set of circumstances.

For example, there were allegations, though in some respects not proven, in relation to the husband regarding –

a   mismanagement of trust assets;

b   threats to deliberately destroy trust property – by way of setting fire to a backpack full of cash, containing more than $4M;

c   creating unnecessary costs (for example, to recover the backpack of cash, the federal police were involved and the bank that took the deposit of the funds charged a processing fee of $15,000);

d   deliberate attempts to mislead the judges through the various stages of the court process;

e   sending letters with suggested draft judgments directly to
High Court judges. While the husband was a lawyer, widely
regarded for his specialisation in relation to trusts, the letters
were considered inappropriate by the court, not least of which
because of their references to matters arguably not relevant to
the case (for example the sexuality and life choices of the High
Court judges).

If you look at Spry in the context of these allegations, in terms of the
wider factual scenario, and some of the subsequent cases, it's probably fair to say that you can distinguish a lot of the general trust structuring planning is in this area, away from the decision of Spry itself.

ESTATE PLANNING IS MORE THAN A WILL

> **"Great minds discuss ideas; average minds discuss events; small minds discuss people."**
>
> — *Eleanor Roosevelt*

Judging books by their cover

Client Scenario

T O THE CASUAL observer, it is probably frustrating that so many ultra high wealth individuals do not appear to be particularly interested in money. Even those who speak about the importance of financial success to them, often suggest that financial success is simply a tool to allow them to achieve a wider dream.

The most financially wealthy family I have assisted over the years also happened to be one of the most purpose driven.

Having initially achieved substantial wealth via a services style business, like so many other high net wealth families, most of the wealth was ultimately diverted into an enormous commercial and residential property portfolio.

Eric and Jan, a husband and wife team, had made it clear to their two daughters and son that only a nominal amount of wealth would pass to them and only when both Eric and Jan had died. To avoid any confusion as to what exactly nominal might mean, Eric and Jan said that each of the children should plan on receiving nothing from the estate.

Perhaps not unexpectedly, given the fantastic success of their parents, each of the children became independently successful in their chosen fields. The two daughters were independently wealthy and the son was recognised as a leader in his chosen profession, although the financial rewards were not as nearly as lucrative as those his sisters enjoyed.

Eric and Jan's self-confessed 'tough love' attitude towards their children (and in due course their grandchildren) was equally evident in a business sense.

The profits earned from the various property investments over the years ultimately dwarfed the substantial wealth that they had earned from the sale of the services business.

Their reputation was generally described as hard, but fair. Others used the word ruthless.

Their approach to the trappings of success was somewhat similar to their estate planning arrangements and somewhat unconventional.

In most (if not all) scenarios of similar wealth, if the family members do not receive the control of the wealth entirely, they at least receive 'beer money' distributions under the estate plan. Sometimes the beer money payments might run to tens of millions of dollars.

There is normally an array of other advantages for family members such as:

a   loans (that are often later forgiven) to allow the purchase of a magnificent family home

b   sums to cover the costs of 'whole of family' holidays, often on a yearly basis, to various exotic locations around the world

c   access to various 'toys', whether they be cars, boats or aircraft

d   substantial financial assistance with costs associated with the raising of the grandchildren.

None of these benefits was afforded to the children here – at least, not in a traditional sense.

In fact, Eric and Jan lived in the same 3-bedroom suburban house that they had acquired as a young married couple before they achieved any financial success.

The rationale for maintaining their primary place of residence, despite the fact that they could have afforded to live in any house, anywhere in the world, was driven by the fact that whenever they were in their base town they would be working, and when they were working, the only thing that they really needed from a house was somewhere to sleep.

They owned many magnificent properties, often retaining prized apartments in various complexes built over the years.

A number of these properties often remained vacant but, when family members used them for holidays, they were charged market rate tariffs.

Neither did the family drive imported cars. Eric and Jan had a driver on 24-hour call but the rationale was simply that, after a long day, it was safer for all concerned not to drive, and it provided better value than constantly using taxis.

Perhaps the single greatest point of difference in terms of Eric and Jan's attitude to wealth, however, was their approach in relation to who would benefit from their wealth.

Countless studies have been done into the attitudes and approaches of high net wealth individuals to charitable and philanthropic giving.

A recurring conclusion in many of these studies is that, for most people, a significant factor in terms of what they choose to do relates to the issue of personal self esteem. In other words, there is a strong desire to receive acknowledgement for their actions.

Obviously, there are numerous other drivers, but the reality is that very few high net wealth individuals maintain complete confidentiality about their contributions to the community.

Eric and Jan ensured complete confidentiality in relation to their charitable giving.

Any charities that received bequests were required to guarantee that they would not publicly declare the source of the bequests.

The family's philanthropic foundation was structured in such a way that no one from the family was directly associated with it, other than to feed it with capital, contributed anonymously.

Through a complex maze of specially crafted companies and trusts, the shares in the ultimate holding company of the business operations would, on Eric and Jan's death, pass to the day-to-day control of the business management team.

The dividends would then flow via the web of structures to the sole benefit of the foundation.

The personal wealth, which was not subject to the same confidentiality driven complexities, was intended to pass to Eric and Jan's grandchildren – again, maintaining complete confidentiality.

The reality was, however, that the wealth represented by these personal assets was less than 1% of the total portfolio, and at least in relation to the children of the two daughters, those grandchildren are ultimately likely to receive more from their parents' estate than they do from Eric and Jan's estate, assuming that the daughters adopt a more traditional approach under their estate plans.

The unwavering discipline with which Eric and Jan have approached all aspects of their business life has been replicated by their attitude to managing the financial returns from the business.

At various junctures, Eric and Jan have endured quite harsh assessments of their approach from immediate family members.

Certainly, countless business associates and external observers have judged Eric and Jan extremely harshly, both in terms of how they appear not to spend any of their wealth on themselves and, just as perversely, do not seem to spend it on any one else either.

At times, the feedback has been at best unflattering and at worse vicious, and designed to cause as much damage as possible.

At no stage, however, have Eric and Jan diverted from the approach that they believe has the best prospects of achieving their goals.

While there are numerous lessons that can be learned from this couple, perhaps the most important is this: I have never seen or heard them pass judgement on the approach that anyone else takes to the management and allocation of financial wealth.

Their purpose is, I believe, right for them and they never assume that it is of any particular use to anyone else.

Court Decision

A standard 'gift and loan back' approach normally involves the owner of an asset gifting an amount equal to their equity in the property or shares in a company to a family trust (or low risk spouse).

The family trust then lends an amount of money to the owner and takes a secured mortgage over the property or registers a security interest on the Personal Property Securities Register over the shares.

The approach effectively removes value from an individual's personal asset portfolio, thereby removing the wealth from being ultimately regulated by the person's will.

Using property as an example, assume that Anne is an 'at risk' person (eg in business) and owns 100% of an investment property and the current value of the property is $1,500,000. There is an existing mortgage of $500,000 owing to her financier.

Step 1: Anne gifts the amount of her equity in the property to a trust

Step 2: The trust subsequently lends the amount back to Anne and takes security over property.

Arguably, the leading case in relation to gift and loan back arrangements is Atia v Nusbaum [2011] QSC044.

In summary the circumstances of this case were as follows:

(1) Dr Atia (a cosmetic surgeon) entered into a gift and loan back style arrangement with his mother;

(2) when Dr Atia's mother subsequently called in the debt, Dr Atia argued that the loan and mortgage were not intended to be actually binding and were only a pretence to protect against situations where Dr Atia was sued professionally;

(3) in particular, Dr Atia argued that his mother was only calling in the debt secured by the mortgage because he had married his girlfriend against his mother's express wishes;

(4) the court found that all aspects of the legal documentation, including a deed of gift, loan agreement and registered mortgage, had been validly signed; and

(5) the court confirmed that the legal effect of the documentation signed was exactly as the parties intended it to be and there was no mistake or sham involved. This meant that Dr Atia's mother was allowed to enforce recoverability of the debt, and if necessary, exercise her rights under the registered mortgage.

While there are a myriad of potential issues that always need to be considered in relation to any gift and loan back arrangement, some of the key aspects include:

(1) care should always be taken to ensure that the trust which will make the secured loan does not itself conduct risky activities (for example, run a business).

(2) while the arrangement can be entered into without registering a mortgage, if this step is not taken, the trust that has made the loan will simply be an unsecured creditor.

(3) the impact of the arrangement in relation to potentially accessing the small business tax concessions should always be carefully considered, because while a family home will generally be excluded from the $6 million test, a secured loan will generally be included if the trust is an affiliate or 'connected entity' under the Tax Act (which will typically be the case).

(4) to the extent that a third party financier already has a mortgage over the property, they will generally require a deed of priority securing their lendings (to whatever level they may be from time to time) as a first priority before the trust's second mortgage.

(5) As flagged in previous posts if no real property is available for registering security over, personal property can be used via the Personal Property Security Register.

(6) Part of strategy ultimately derives from the (in)famous Dr Geoffrey Edelstein (see - the case of Max Christopher Donnelly As Trustee of the Bankrupt Estate of Geoffrey Walter Edelsten v Geoffrey Walter Edelsten and Ors [1994] FCA 992).

Michael Hutchence (singer of popular 1980s band 'INXS') is another high profile person who is thought to have utilised the gift & loan back strategy. This said, his will is sealed by the Supreme Court of Queensland (i.e. not available for review) and there is no related documentation publically available making it difficult to know with certainty how he had structured his arrangements.

This said, Hutchence's estimated fortune at time of his death was $10-20 million.

There were claims from his advisers that he did not want his 'thieving relatives' or ex-girlfriends getting his estate and that had assisted Hutchence to structure his arrangements to achieve this outcome.

In contrast, a number of family members (although some claimants were at best 'distant', if not estranged) argued that this was at odds as to what was in his will, although this cannot be confirmed because as noted, the will is sealed.

Arguably the case is an example of another rule of law, namely 'where there is a will there is a relative'.

In July 2005, lawyers (Hong Kong firm Boase Cohen and Collins) valued Hutchence's estate at $1078:

(1) $506 cash;
(2)   Share of INXS's bank account $572.

The estate sold assets such as artwork, guitars; a Harley Davidson and a Jeep car.

Outgoings of the estate included $670,000 in legal fees as well as other outgoings.

Not included in the estate were the following assets that it was claimed Michael owned:

a   3 Gold Coast Properties (at 2005 valued around $10 million);
b   Villa in France;
c   House in Chelsea (London);
d   Indonesian development;
e   Various luxury cars; and
f   Continuing INXS royalties.

Michael was known for having structured financial affairs through the British Virgin Islands, Liberia and the Caribbean (known tax havens).

His royalties are allegedly held by a trust known as the 'Vocals Trust' of which he was not a beneficiary.

Gordon Fisher, a Monaco based tax adviser wrote to the lawyers administering the estate who said Vocals was an 'asset protection trust' for protection against (as noted above) 'thieving relatives', ex-girlfriends and future wives.

A lot of the assets thought to have been 'owned' by Michael were in fact 'owned' on paper by his business advisers.

While there is no clear indication, it seems apparent Michael used a more complex version of a 'gift and loan back arrangement'.

It was also reported that the family sued Michael's advisers. However it is believed the matter was settled out of court.

It appears the family did not recover the costs that were in-excess (no pun intended) of $500,000, incurred in their failed attempts to challenge the estate.

Michael's mother told the press at the conclusion of the litigation that 'I got a couple of small bowls, some awards, and a big poster of Brigitte Bardot in 'And God Created Woman'.'

Fifth Principle

DON'T GET STUCK IN THE MIDDLE

> **Leaders volunteer to go first into danger. Their willingness to sacrifice for us is the reason we are inspired to follow.**
>
> — *Simon Sinek*

Lost and found

Client Scenario

FOR DECADES, MOST lawyers have charged on the basis of six-minute increments multiplied by an hourly rate.

Such a pricing model can lead to all manner of adverse outcomes for a client, and there are many lawyers that have earned particular reputations via strategies, such as:

a   'Rush hour' – trying to perform as many tasks that take fewer than 6 minutes as possible, in an hour, knowing that the computer systems deem everything to have lasted for at least 6 minutes. In some cases, this can mean 2 hours of chargeable time recorded in any 1-hour block

b   'Nearest whole hour' – under this methodology, any task that takes at least 30 minutes is rounded up to a full hour, again potentially delivering exponential returns

c   'Parallel plains' – this strategy involves charging one client for travel time while working on another client's file.

There are countless other time billing related 'war stories'. Many of these were the catalysts for ensuring that the part of the legal firm I was responsible for replaced time-based billing with upfront guaranteed fixed pricing in 2004.

Before then, while we had always given estimates, often they were calculated almost entirely with reference to the time a particular task would take, regardless of the actual value delivered to the client.

For example, particular tasks would often be redone from scratch, without any leveraging off previous learnings. In cases where a client's other advisers (such as accountants or financial advisers) might have had information that would make our work significantly quicker or easier, a client would invariably sense that we had not paid sufficient regard to it and therefore would look to test every aspect of the information.

This meant that we had perhaps two to four meetings to deal with issues which, if we worked more collaboratively with existing advisers, we might actually have been able to address in just one.

This said, additional meetings often created an environment where issues could be explored more deeply, and a led to the sharing of a number of the stories or anecdotes mentioned in this book.

The genesis of this story, *Lost and Found,* is from before 2004. Not unusually, there had been three meetings and I still remember thinking, during the first two, how privileged I was to spend time with such a famous couple, named here as Norman and Christine, as inspirational in person as their significant media profile suggested.

The first meeting focused on getting an understanding of the client circumstances, including:

a   the couple's marriage
b   the children – a son aged 34 and a daughter aged 31; one grandchild to the daughter
c   a range of assets accumulated during the course of the marriage, including a family home, investment property and superannuation savings.

The second meeting dealt with the development of the estate plan and the instructions regarding various aspects of it.

The third meeting was largely to arrange the signing of estate planning documents.

During the second (and easily the longest) meeting, Norman and Christine worked through their preferred outcomes on a number of issues, particularly determining at what point in time their two children would gain control of the wealth.

To help guide the clients on this matter, I related a situation I had seen some years earlier.

An ultra high net wealth couple in their early 70s had decided to prohibit all of their five children from gaining access to assets until the year 2025. Using the whiteboard to highlight the point, I had explained to the couple that setting the relevant date at 2025 would mean that even the youngest of their five children would be over 80 – even older than the couple was at the time – before any of the children had access to assets.

I challenged the couple as to whether they really did want to create that scenario. They asked me to leave the room while they considered what was appropriate, and when I returned around five minutes later, they thanked me and agreed that they had not thought deeply enough about the age at which each of their five children would be responsible enough to manage the wealth. They resolved, instead that the year would not be 2025, but rather 2030 – in other words, any attempt to encourage them to allow earlier access to wealth had failed so badly that the clients had decided to *increase* the waiting period!

Just as critically, the couple had resolved that they would keep all aspects of their estate planning entirely secret from their children until after their death.

When the couple ultimately died, one of their children had already passed away and another passed away shortly after.

The three remaining children, who had never known their parents' intentions, were completely bewildered by what had happened, and litigation commenced against the executors of the estate. The executors (who were based offshore) decided, amongst other things, that in order to understand the nature of each asset, they should fly around the world, first class, to inspect properties owned by the estate, as well as attend shareholders' meetings of the dozens of global companies in which the estate owned shares.

More than $1 million of executor fees were incurred in the first three months of the administration of the estate and the fees escalated as the litigation progressed.

The point of sharing the couple's story with Norman and Christine was that, while it is certainly possible to rule from the grave, if that is the intention, it would be better, during their lifetime, to position the approach with the people involved; because once you are gone, it is obviously too late.

For Norman and Christine, in relation to their two children, the 'communication is the key' principle became the catalyst for a fundamental change in their overall estate plan; it started towards the end of the third meeting, which had been intended simply to review of the relevant documentation and arrange for it to be signed. The meeting lasted for less than 30 minutes and the clients decided to go to lunch.

As we walked out through reception, Christine asked to be excused. She went to the restroom and Norman and I waited in a long, narrow corridor adjacent to the building's lift well. Having discussed the restaurant booking and the weather, there was a long pause. Then Norman asked rather bluntly, 'Would it make any difference to my estate plan if I told you I had a son – who is now 33; I have only recently re-established contact with him and am starting to build a fairly close relationship'.

Before I could respond, Christine rejoined us in the corridor and we walked towards the lift. My parting comment to Norman as he stepped into the lift was, 'We should probably catch up at some stage, when you are ready'.

What transpired in the subsequent discussions was that Norman had been agonising over what to do about his 33-year old secret.

The estate planning process had highlighted an overwhelming desire to avoid causing difficulties from the grave. He was almost certain that unless he found a way to communicate with his wife of 37 years and their two children, their inevitable anguish later would probably overshadow was what an otherwise unblemished relationship with him as husband and father.

After further agonising, Norman decided on a full disclosure to Christine and their two children, but only by way of a series of heartfelt clauses in his will – clauses that would remain secret until after his death.

The result of this approach was that after Norman's death the anger and resentment felt by Christine and their two children led to litigation that rivalled the intensity (if not the costs) of any case.

There is no way of knowing if the outcome might have been different but Norman's failure to communicate about his 'lost son', during his lifetime, guaranteed that what had otherwise been an inspirational life story, was destroyed irretrievably for those who mattered most.

Technical Example

Rather then explore court decisions, for this chapter we will consider one issue that comes up regularly in estate planning exercises where there is more than one family unit ultimately to benefit–that is whether single or multiple testamentary trusts (**TT**s) should be implemented.

For example, if there are three adult children, each to share an estate, should those three children jointly control a single TT or should each child (perhaps with a co-trustee) control a separate TT, with each TT receiving one-third of the estate.

As with many aspects of estate planning, there is no 'correct' approach. This said, some of the factors that would tend to support using a single TT include:

(1)   if some (or all) of the children are under the age of 18 – an estate planning exercise should always be undertaken on the assumption that the willmaker dies shortly after signing the document. Therefore the primary focus should be on the needs of the surviving spouse. In these circumstances, it is generally not appropriate for the wealth to be held across multiple TTs where the surviving spouse will likely be in control for many years;

(2)   if asset protection (for example guarding against a relationship breakdown of any of the children) is critical, then generally a single TT will be the more robust approach;

(3)   if the vision of the will maker is to have the next generation (i.e. their children) effectively act as 'custodian' for future

generations, then this is normally more easily achieved via a single trust; and

(4)   if the underlying nature of the assets would make a 'split' ownership structure unduly complicated – for example if there is, say, one significant asset (such a property or business).

There are a wide range of the factors that might be relevant in deciding to implement multiple TTs. Many of these factors have a practical focus and can include:

(1)   the different geographical locations of the children – particularly if one or more children live overseas;

(2)   poor relationships between siblings (or their respective spouses) meaning that jointly controlling wealth is likely to further fragment family dynamics;

(3)   the risk profiles of each child's investment outlook;

(4)   the underlying nature of the wealth – for example, if particular assets are earmarked for the sole control of a particular beneficiary;

(5)   differences in the 'life cycle' of each beneficiary – for example if one child themselves has young (or no) children whereas another child has adult children, their investment objectives can look quite different;

(6)   the desire to have different control mechanisms in relation to different children – for example one child might be the sole controller of their TT whereas another child may have one or more co-trustees, or indeed, not be a trustee at all; and

(7)   there can be a myriad of difficulties that arise if a single TT is utilised and it is still running in, say, two generations time both in terms of overall management of the structure and how income and capital is ultimately allocated.

One mechanism that we have seen used with increasing regularity is a 'hybrid' approach. Under this model, elements of both the single and multiple testamentary trust solutions are combined.

For example:

(1)　control of this 'head' trust is jointly shared amongst various family members and any nominated independent trustees;

(2)　a separate TT is also established for each child and their respective lineal descendants;

(3)　a separate percentage share of the estate, or discreet assets, are then gifted to each of these 'sub' TTs; and

(4)　normally each child would control (perhaps jointly with a co-trustee) 'their' TT. Each child would also have the ability to independently regulate succession of control for their trust.

As in any estate planning exercise the appropriateness of the hybrid approach will depend on a range of issues including the exact objectives of the client, the overall family dynamics and the nature and value of the wealth involved.

Ultimately however the most important principle is to remember the flow on lyric after the refrain 'clowns to the left of me, jokers to the right' and not get 'stuck in the middle'. In other words, ensure that a decision is made and a will incorporating at least one TT is implemented in a timely manner, if TTs are appropriate.

Sixth Principle

MURPHY'S LAW

66 **Never doubt that a small group of committed citizens can change the world. Indeed, it's the only thing that ever has.** 99

— *Margaret Mead*

The Last Flight to Fiji

Client Scenario

FOR MANY YEARS, a key message in estate planning seminars has been the mantra 'even if you don't have an estate plan, you have an estate plan'.

The underlying theme being that Murphy's Law often happens when most inconvenient and least expected.

When it does, the consequences can be life changing and often traumatic for those involved.

People who plan for the worst while hoping for the best, like preparing for war in times of peace, often avoid disaster.

The success of many modern law firms is to a large extent due to the fact that most people, most of the time, avoid addressing the issues that, in hindsight, they often wish they had.

One very powerful example of this principle in practice relates to the significant tax advantages that are available on death, as long as appropriate estate plan steps are implemented prior to a person actually passing away.

There is significant literature explaining the technical aspects of the tax benefits, which is outside the scope of this book. Largely, the philosophy derives from the concept that, at least in Australia, death is not a tax-planning event.

In very limited circumstances, it is possible to 'reverse engineer' many of the tax benefits after somebody's death and, for many years, the Fiji pilot story provided just one example of how this can help.

The story itself has a broad framework similar to that of dozens of other stories that give rise to the same solution:

a   the person central to the story is too young; in situations I have seen firsthand, the youngest person has been 24, the oldest 42 b   the person dying leaves dependants – usually a spouse and children under the age of 18

c   the dependants are left under financial duress because of the death – there is insufficient wealth, even after insurance and superannuation payments, to maintain a lifestyle comparable to that enjoyed before the death

d   tn the vast majority of cases the central person is male.

The circumstances of the death include accidents involving cars, bicycles, motorcycles, planes, and helicopters, water related incidents, heart attacks, cancer, brain aneurysms, suicide and murder.

So that each presentation remains as 'fresh' as possible, I will often select stories involving these events, at random.

I will also make sure that the significant parts of a story are varied, so as to disassociate them from real client situations.

This story – *The Last flight to Fiji* – involves a young couple Daniel and Marie-Louise, who had met by chance in far North Queensland about five years earlier.

Daniel was a commercial pilot who primarily flew commercial helicopters out of both Townsville and Fiji. Marie-Louise was a marketing consultant who, at the time they met, was on a 3-month contract with the department of tourism.

After a courtship of around two years, and after living in Townsville for 18 months, Marie-Louise became pregnant with their first child.

Having been disciplined with savings, and having pooled their funds, the young couple had accumulated enough wealth not only to buy their 'dream home' on Queensland's Sunshine Coast, about two hours north of Brisbane, but also to take 12 months off work after the birth of their child.

They both officially 'retired' from work, three months before the due date, so they could settle into their new home and community.

Based on the photos I saw, Daniel had ruggedly good looks – with a mop of blonde hair, blue eyes and olive skin – much in the style of Robert Redford. I never met him because, about six weeks before the due date of his daughter's birth, he received a phone call from the cargo company he had worked for in Townsville, asking him to help out on a handful of flights that the owners believed would help secure a new, substantial, customer for the company, in Fiji.

As things had gone so well with the move into the new house and the pregnancy, Marie-Louise encouraged Daniel to help his former employers, and the first few flights were uneventful.

The third flight, however, was to be his last.

The storm activity that Daniel encountered about 20 minutes off the coast of Fiji had not been on any radar reports prior to take off. By the time the helicopter disappeared from air traffic control radar, the storm activity was so severe that all other flights that day were cancelled.

The wreckage from the helicopter was never located.

On receiving the news of her husband's death, Marie-Louise went into an immediate and very traumatic labour and both she and her daughter (born six weeks premature) spent a number of weeks in hospital.

By the time I met her about two years later, Marie-Louise was as stunningly attractive as I imagined she had been when she met her late husband. She had naturally blonde shoulder length hair, ocean blue eyes, with the physique of a ballerina. I still recall the attention that she drew from the clients in reception on the morning I met her for the first time.

Despite her stunning physical appearance, emotionally she was spent. By her own admission, she had barely slept a night since first learning of Daniel's death, and certainly had not worked or even thought about working since.

Unless she carefully managed the balance of Daniel's life insurance policy payout, Marie-Louise might be forced to sell her dream home simply to ensure that there would be sufficient food on the table.

My rather academic role was to work in conjunction with her accountant to help establish a special form of trust that would provide sufficient tax benefits, in relation to the insurance payout, to delay (and ideally avoid) the need to sell the family home.

And that, until one night four years later in Sydney, was the end of the story.

On the night in question, I had included the story as part of a 45-minute seminar, delivered to a group of high net wealth individuals invited by the financial planners in a private banking arm of one of the big four banks.

It is usual for a number of the attendees stay behind after the formal presentation to ask questions directly relevant to their circumstances. For reasons which I never take personally, it is rare for someone to be the *only* one left in the room – with a lawyer.

This particular evening, however, one woman waited until everyone else had left and, after introducing herself as Amy, commented that my use of stories throughout the presentation had been a very effective way to reinforce a number of messages.

As I began methodically to pack up the equipment, Amy remarked bluntly, "You should make sure, though, that you change your stories enough so that people cannot work out who you are actually talking about".

As I slightly fumbled with the power cord, my reflex verbal response tried to disguise that sinking feeling in my stomach. "Well", I said, "I always do".

"Tonight you didn't, Matthew".

"Yes, well, everything was deliberately mixed up bit as usual, as I remember", I responded in rapid fire. I felt the need to pack up quickly and be out of the auditorium immediately.

As I picked up the laptop bag and moved to shake Amy's hand and thank her for attending, her tear-filled eyes caught mine and she whispered, "Matthew, I was the one who phoned your pilot".

The long silence that followed was broken as Amy repeated, "Matthew, I was the one who phoned your pilot to ask for his help. I was the one who caused his death". It's not just his widow who hasn't been able to sleep since that day. She sees the face of her husband.

I see the faces of Daniel, Marie-Louise and their beautiful young daughter. The post script is that the tax savings that your fancy legal work delivered only enabled Marie-Louise to inject illicit substances into her forearms, thighs and under her toenails. She hasn't lost her life yet, but she has lost her daughter to the state government and her house to her creditors".

Amy went on, "While you might think that Sydney is a long way away from Brisbane and Brisbane is a long way away from Fiji, always, always, always make sure that you honour those absent and protect their privacy when you are sharing your stories".

Having made her point so compellingly, Amy then took the time to explain to me the personal journey she had taken towards a greater understanding of what it means to influence and inspire one's self, as well as others.

Perhaps most pointedly, she explained something that many insightful leaders seem to know; of all the things that you do, some can have influence and some cannot. The critical learning is understanding the difference between the two.

Amy had spent some time trying to help the family that she felt she had influenced adversely, but when it became clear that they had no interest in what she had to offer, her energy was channelled into three areas and, in each, she had created significant positive change.

In her own family, there had been significant health issues with an adult daughter, and with complete unselfishness, Amy had devoted time, energy and resources to address them.

In the cargo business, losing two pilots and a helicopter would potentially bring catastrophic personal and financial trauma to a medium size business. In fact, business doubled within four years of the accident, creating significant opportunities for all those associated with it.

Finally, much of the additional profit generated by the sustained growth was used to make significant improvements to pilot training and overall air safety for all aircraft operating in Fijian airspace.

Court Decision

The case involving the family of famous retailer Solomon Lew (Lew), in Solomon Lew & Ors v Adam Priester & Ors [2012] VSC 57 is a useful of how plans can unravel.

Broadly the situation was as follows –

a   Based on tax advice about an impending tax change (which was ultimately never implemented), certain distributions were made by a trust ultimately controlled by Lew to each of his children

b   The potential change was proposed in the late 1990's and was known as the 'profits first rule' which would have seen a mandatory requirement that any distribution from a trust would presumed to be of profits and therefore taxable.

c   2 of Lew's children some years later were caught up in (separate) property settlements following the breakdown of their respective marriages.

d   The former spouses claimed the outstanding loans were assets of Lew's children and therefore able to be subject to orders of the Family Court.

e   Lew argued that his children did not have any beneficial interest in the loan accounts due to agreements entered which resulted in the amounts in fact being held by the children on a trust for Lew and his wife Rose.

While the exact outcome as to whether the loans were in fact assets of the children appears to be unknown (it is assumed the cases must have settled out of court or the decisions de-identified), the fact that the former spouses were able to mount the arguments is a reminder that the wider commercial implications of any tax planning strategy should always be considered carefully.

Here, as in many estate planning 'fails', a unifying principle is Murphy's Law – that is anything that can go wrong, will.

Seventh Principle

ITERATE AND UPDATE

> **When the rate of change outside exceeds the rate of change inside, the end is near.**
>
> — *Jack Welch*

Failing to plan

Client Scenario

N THE EARLY 1990s, one group of visionary dentists developed an aggregation business model that set an industry benchmark in terms of the growth enjoyed.

Indeed, the growth rates were so impressive that the success of the model seemed virtually guaranteed.

While each of the five principals behind the business model were intelligent and successful professionals in their own right, the reality was that in many respects, their business was in fact a start-up enterprise.

As is the case with many start-ups, the entrepreneurial spirit that often drives initial success and growth can just as easily be the catalyst for difficulties to arise. In this business, what otherwise seemed to be an innocuous decision made very early in the lifecycle ultimately proved to be the sole reason for the business' ultimate failure.

Not long after the five principal owners agreed to pool their resources and commit totally to the aggregation model that they had been working on, in one form or another, for a number of years, the accountant for the new venture recommended that, as part of the process of formalising the arrangements between the parties, a written partnership agreement should be entered into.

The business owners, like many in a similar situation, did not see the investment of significant energy into reviewing and agreeing the specific terms of the partnership agreement as a particularly useful exercise. This attitude was primarily driven by three factors:

a   each partner felt that if there were to be serious problems between them in the short term, then they would all just simply go their separate ways. They could implement a proper partnership agreement in, perhaps, three years' time if the business proved to be successful

b   an investment into a comprehensive partnership agreement at this stage was likely to be a significant distraction from what they all saw as a priority – developing and growing the business

c   they believed that a partnership agreement was probably only of interest to the accountants and lawyers and therefore, it should be for them to drive the process, not the dentists themselves.

The accountant was, therefore, left to source the appropriate document and arrange for it to be signed.

Seeing firsthand the dentists' lack of interest in having any form of agreement at this stage, the accountant decided, probably insightfully, that the simplest approach would be to buy a template document and fill in the missing details rather than risking any form of protracted negotiations.

In conjunction with the partnership agreement, the accountant also convinced the partners to take out life insurance policies, designed to enable the exit of a partner's estate if one were to die unexpectedly.

In order to maintain flexibility and maximise the tax effectiveness of the insurance funded arrangements, the principals acquired a policy over their own lives that would be paid to their estates if they were to pass away.

The exiting estate would simply be released from all the external financier obligations on the sale of their deceased spouse's partnership interest for a dollar.

While this arrangement was never formally documented, there was evidence to suggest that, at a dinner party involving all partners and their respective spouses, it was discussed at length, particularly why each spouse should have been comfortable in selling a partnership interest for a dollar, on the basis that the insurance company would have paid them $1 million.

At the time the arrangements were put in place, the $1 million insurance policy represented a payout that was, even on an aggressive valuation of the underlying partnership interest, at least fourfold the value of each partner's interest.

Over the following six years, the business grew exponentially, and by the time one of the founding partners suffered a fatal heart attack, just shy of his 43rd birthday, each partner's interest was worth in the region of $1.8 million.

The need to revisit the legal agreements between the partners had remained as a standing agenda item at each year's partner's retreat. It had never been progressed.

This said, as far as the surviving four partners were concerned, the process that needed to be followed was quite clear:

a   the insurance company would make the $1 million payment to the exiting partner's spouse

b   the surviving partners would release the spouse from all liabilities of the business

c   the surviving spouse would transfer the estate's partnership interest to the surviving four partners for one dollar.

Given that none of the partners had revisited the quantum of their insurance cover, the four remaining partners were open to paying an additional amount to the spouse of the deceased partner – somewhere in the region of $350,000. The rationale for the discount (an effective total of $1.35 million, compared with $1.8 million) was that while there might have been a number of buyers for the entire partnership, realistically there were very few buyers who would be keen to acquire a one fifth interest.

Furthermore, given the deceased partner had not taken steps to review his insurance cover, there should be some discount applied.

Melissa, the spouse of the deceased partner saw things somewhat differently.

As a starting point, she felt that the $1.8 million valuation was unduly conservative. Melissa had advice that indicated that it was based solely on historical earnings and did not factor in the realistic expected growth of the business.

Melissa also argued that if the partners had really intended for a deceased estate to sell its partnership interest for one dollar, then this should have been documented in writing. The fact that it was not meant that she did not consider herself bound. In other words, the $1 million payout she received was effectively just compensation for the fact that her husband had died. She would, therefore, retain the one fifth partnership interest until the remaining partners acquired the interest at market value, which was at least $1.8 million.

Melissa's arguments were difficult to refute, and not just because of the lack of written agreement in relation to the insurance proceeds.

While the default legal position is that the death of a partner automatically terminates any partnership, this position can be varied by written agreement.

Generally speaking, on the death of a partner, the estate is immediately removed from the partnership because of the instantaneous termination, but if there is a written agreement that the partnership remains on foot, then the executors of that deceased estate will themselves become a partner in the partnership.

The partnership agreement that the accountant had organised some six years earlier had very few substantive provisions to it, other than a clause, buried at the end of the document, which stated that the death of any partner did not terminate the partnership.

In other words, Melissa was now, in her position as executor of her late husband's estate, a one fifth partner in the partnership, and there was no legal right to force her exit, if she chose not to sell.

What followed were almost three years of legal arguments. A settlement was finally reached, literally on the steps of the courtroom, on the first day of what would have otherwise been a 5-day trial.

The legal and accounting costs were already substantial and the settlement left all parties largely dissatisfied.

In broad terms, the remaining four partners agreed to pay Melissa an additional $450,000 plus her legal costs of almost $300,000. They also were required to pay their own legal fees.

In return, Melissa agreed to exit as a partner and not claim any account of profits from the earnings of the partnership for the three years during which she was in fact a partner.

The true costs for the ongoing partners were significantly more after taking into account the opportunity costs incurred and the distraction from actually running the business during the 3-year litigation process.

Within six weeks of the settlement, however, it was as if nothing had been resolved. As is the case with virtually every professional practice in Australia, the dentists' partnership was not the only entity involved in operating the business.

A company, owned by five trusts (one for the benefit of each of the dentists' families) provided substantial services to the partnership, pursuant to arm's length terms; the company derived substantial profits from its operations.

In the process of crafting the settlement arrangements with Melissa, no steps had been taken to secure ownership of the shares in the service company.

Whether Melissa and her advisers had deliberately not raised the issue as part of the initial settlement proceedings or had themselves not discovered the existence of the company until the initial settlement had been finalised was never resolved.

In many respects, the answer to that question became academic. It was clear that Melissa, via control of the discretionary trust, was entitled to one fifth of all the company's profits for the three years since her husband's death.

It was also clear that in order to prevent the trust from having an ongoing entitlement to one fifth of all profits, a further negotiated settlement would be required.

After some weeks of additional negotiation, an additional payment of approximately $400,000 was made by the remaining partners to secure their former partner's shares in the service company.

While ultimately the business survived the trauma of failing to invest in appropriate agreements, their growth trajectory effectively stagnated for over three years while they fought to regain full control of the business.

They eventually implemented agreements that addressed all of the issues that had caused them so much difficulty, but the unavoidable conclusion was that it was too little, too late.

Within two years of the final settlement payment, the partnership was wound up, when a competitor firm, replicating almost identically the partners' original business model, took what the partners perceived to be an unassailable lead in the aggregation race.

Court Decision

The saga involving swimmer Grant Hackett suing two law firms for negligence is a high profile reminder of the difficulties in relation to 'pre-nups'.

Broadly the Hackett matter centred on allegations that the relevant law firms failed to properly advise him to create a binding financial agreement.

In particular, Hackett argued that the original agreement entered into before marriage failed to comply with the strict legal requirements under the Family Law Act. When the agreement was later updated after the birth of the couple's twin children the alleged difficulties with the agreement were not remedied.

In many respects the issues here are analogous to the relatively well known 'pole dancer' case of Wallace v Stelzer [2014] HCATrans 135 - so named because the husband met the wife at what was described as 'an adult entertainment venue' where the wife was working as a pole dancer.

At the heart of the pole dancer case was the husband's desire to avoid the terms of the binding financial agreement that saw him liable to pay $3 million to his former wife when their marriage ended after only 18 months.

Some of the arguments raised included that the lawyers failed to discharge their duty to properly explain the terms of the agreement - an allegation that would have seen the lawyers potentially liable in negligence if it had been held to be correct.

It was also argued that the agreement was void in relation to some technical aspects required to be complied with under the Family Law Act and that attempted legislative fixes to the rules were also invalid, in part because the changes purported to be retrospective.

While it was ultimately held that the agreement was effective and the legislative changes were valid the extent of the litigation has seen many law firms, even those that specialise solely in family law, choose to no longer prepare binding financial agreements.

Another relevant decision is Hills v Chalk & Ors (as executors of the estate of Chalk (deceased)) [2008] QCA 159. The case is important because it starkly highlights the importance of regularly iterating and updating an estate plan – as well as the potential significance of a Binding Financial Agreement (**BFA**) even where the BFA does not comply with the Family Law Act.

In this case, Mr Hills and Mrs Chalk entered into a 'pre-nuptial' agreement in 1994, which was before the ability to make an enforceable BFA. The terms of the pre-nuptial agreement were essentially contractually based and provided that in the event of their separation, they were each to retain their own assets and make no claim for property settlement, or maintenance from the other.

The agreement also recorded a joint intention to preserve their assets for their respective families. Importantly, they acknowledged that each party should not seek to defeat the intention of the other.

Mrs Chalk died in February 2003, and probate was granted in April 2003 to the children of Mrs Chalk. In September 2007, some 4 years after her death, Mr Hills made an application for further provision from the deceased estate.

In her will, Mrs Chalk had given Mr Hills a right to reside in her house, and a legacy of $20,000 in recognition of him caring for her during illness. The balance of her estate was left to her children.

The court refused Mr Hills' application stating it was 'distinctly improbable' that Mrs Chalk had failed to make adequate provision for Mr Hills.

In particular, it was held that the 'pre-nuptial' agreement made by the parties, although not of itself directly decisive against Mr Hills' claim, was of significance to the assessment to be made by the court of Mr Hills' application for further provision.

Following the decision in this case it is generally accepted that a BFA, perhaps even if not binding for Family Law purposes, will generally be taken into account in any claim for further provision from an estate.

Eighth Principle

JUST DO IT

"Man sacrifices his health in order to make money. Then he sacrifices money to recuperate his health. And then he is so anxious about the future that he does not enjoy the present; the result being that he does not live in the present or the future; he lives as if he is never going to die, and then dies having never really lived. "

— *Dalai Lama*

Beating the rule of three

Client Scenario

THE 'RAGS TO rags in three generations' rule states that:

    a   the first generation in the family makes the money (goes from rags to riches)

    b   the second generation holds or keeps the money

    c   the third generation loses the money (goes back to rags).

There are countless proofs of this rule, even in Australia, where the concept of 'old money' has none of the history that the phrase evokes in Europe, or for that matter, in the United States.

An increasing number of high net wealth Australian families seem to be focused on ensuring that the rule is at least delayed, in relation to their family, for a further generation, if not for longer.

Part of the prevailing mindset seems to be driven, or at least inspired, by Warren Buffett, who said: '*A very rich person should leave their kids enough to do anything, but not enough to do nothing*'.

Adopting a holistic attitude to the concept of investing was probably more publicly popularised by the Packer family. As the story goes, both Kerry and James were sent by their respective fathers on accelerated life learning journeys that were specifically designed to empower them with experiences and skills that would provide them with the ability to be successful in managing significant wealth.

Methods and resources vary significantly between families, as does the emphasis placed on various aspects of potential investment. In recent years, however, a methodical approach to ensuring that the next generation is at least able to maintain, if not grow, accumulated resources is rapidly becoming the rule, rather than the exception.

The model developed by one high net wealth family, that has proved to be extremely successful so far, provides an interesting case study of what investment means.

This particular family has a history of land related entrepreneurship across three generations, although admittedly in seemingly unrelated areas.

The family's initial wealth, which was not particularly substantial at the time, was made during the 1960s and '70s, when the father of one of our clients ran a road transport distribution business across the eastern seaboard.

While in his early 30s, our client Mark took over the business in the early 1980s, when his father passed away unexpectedly, and while there had been no succession plan in place, the handover occurred relatively seamlessly.

Arguably due more to luck than design, our client sold the business in the mid 1980s and used most of the proceeds to buy a handful of mining tenements in western New South Wales.

Having failed for about 10 years to get any project off the ground, and having virtually exhausted all funds from the sale of the transport business, he started construction on a new mining project in 1996 and it was fully operational by the time the mining boom was gathering pace in the late 1990s and early 2000s.

Selling out, at the top of the market in the mid 2000s, to one of the larger mining firms, again due to good luck, Mark invested virtually all the proceeds into cattle farming operations at a time when his two daughters Jane and Isobel were finishing their formal schooling and considering what they would do next.

The wealth generated from the sale of the mining interest was of a quantum that meant that even if the funds were simply put in a term deposit, no family member would need to work for at least two generations.

Some years after the start of the estate planning exercise, the two daughters still do not have a full appreciation of the quantum of the wealth. This fact does not appear to have changed either their, or their parents', attitude to the importance of the process that has been developed.

While both daughters indicated a preference for working in the family business as soon as they became aware of the farms being acquired, Mark decided that neither his own children nor those of any subsequent generation, would work in the family business until they had reached the age of 30 years.

Effectively, this forced both Jane and Isobel to find their own pathways in their formative years.

Apart from the expense of one tertiary degree for each of his daughters, Mark paid none of their expenses.

Mark encouraged a 'gap' year but this was not to be financially supported, other than in relation to volunteer activities in indigenous communities in outback Australia. Both daughters participated voluntarily in programs that met this definition – Jane for about eight weeks, Isobel for over six months. In return, the daughters received payments effectively equal to award rates in a retail job, based on a 40-hour week.

As both daughters approached their 30th birthdays, still indicating a desire to be more actively involved in the family business, they were required to apply formally for positions that they felt best reflected their respective skill sets.

Because they both hoped to take on positions of responsibility inside the organisation, particularly if either or both of their parents were unable to act, they were encouraged to complete relevant courses, such as programs with the Australian Institute of Company Directors.

The family established a 'shadow board' of which both Jane and Isobel were members. They were each assigned a mentor director and were required to meet formally for at least one hour before each 'real' board meeting, which they attended as guests and observers. Over time, on topics that were directly related to their area of responsibility as employees, they were required to present to the board.

Eventually, as the prospect of their becoming fully fledged board members became more likely, they became heavily involved in working with the board to develop position descriptions that would apply not only to them, but also to future generations of board members.

Jane and Isobel were also intimately involved in the crafting and ultimate implementation of their parents' estate planning arrangements. This involved numerous meetings with relevant professional advisers as well as a meticulous process that analysed how each aspect of the family's wealth would be transferred on the death or incapacity of either or both of their parents.

Importantly, this exercise involved the implementation of complementary estate planning arrangements for each of Jane and Isobel and, because by this stage they were married, for their respective spouses.

In order for Jane and Isobel to assume any positions of authority within the group, it was a prerequisite that they each have binding financial agreements (or prenups) negotiated with their spouses and agreed upon.

This process took over 18 months, and while unquestionably not a particularly pleasant exercise for either of the daughters, it was one that proved critical when Jane endured a relationship breakdown less than four years after finalising the binding financial agreement.

The daughters' growth in skills and confidence throughout this process was impressive, to say the least.

Towards the end of what their parents had intended to be their formal educative journey, Jane and Isobel conceptualised and largely implemented two of the most important estate planning components.

Firstly, they resolved that a family constitution should be developed. This non-legal document was essentially designed for future generations to provide a framework and reference point for the principles that were important to the family. The document touched on topics as diverse as education, access to finance, investment philosophies, the use of alcohol and illicit substances, and gambling.

Secondly, Jane and Isobel worked to establish a charitable foundation that would ultimately be the primary responsibility of non-bloodline family members; – the husbands of the two daughters were both nominated as founding directors of the charity. Part of the rationale for having spouses actively involved in the charitable aspects of the family business was to ensure that they would always have a seat at the table – directly linked to the family business, but unable to undermine or influence decision making in the business itself.

What was probably most powerful about the components outlined above, in terms of the overall succession plan, was that their usefulness was not dependent on the underlying wealth involved.

In other words, most of the ideas are those that any family, no matter what their financial position, could sensibly implement and still achieve most, if not all, of the advantages that this family derived from them.

Court Decision

One famous example of intergenerational wealth transfers of 'doing it early and doing it often' or 'just doing it' is the media family of Murdoch.

Under the estate plan of Keith Murdoch he gave his wife, Dame Elisabeth Murdoch (**Dame**), a life interest in the income of several family trusts settled by him in the 1930s.

The remainder interest was held by one or more of the Dame's children or grandchildren.

For many years, the trustee of the relevant trusts was effectively Dame, her son Rupert Murdoch and a third party.

It was however noted that the Dame was likely influenced in her role to accept the investment decisions of Rupert, no doubt because of his strong personality.

A 'Reorganisation Agreement' was entered into many years after Keith's death. Under the agreement, Dame surrendered her life interests under each of the trusts, in exchange for a lump sum payment of more than $85m.

The payment was couched as releasing the trustees from potential claims for breaches of trustee duties.

In particular, the investment policy that had been adopted (apparently at Rupert's strong recommendation) was overwhelmingly weighted to shares in Murdoch family companies (e.g. News Corp) that produced capital growth, but comparatively small dividend income.

This investment approach essentially benefited the remainder beneficiaries, at the expense of the Dame as life tenant.

The payment was said to be to help avoid the need for litigation amongst the family.

Around 65% of the $85m was then gifted by the Dame to Rupert and charities she was associated with.

The payment was funded by the sale of pre capital gains tax shares and was therefore essentially received tax free by the Dame.

The Tax Office was therefore not particularly impressed and challenged the arrangements (see - Murdoch v FCT [2008] FCAFC 86).

In confirming the extremely onerous fiduciary duties of a trustee the court confirmed that Rupert had breached his obligations, even though there was no lack of good faith or particular damage to the Dame.

The court relied particularly on the principles of the case Phipps v Boardman [1967] 2 AC 26, which held that this style of claim was not for a reimbursement of the income shortfall.

The payment was therefore on capital, not income, account as a claim against the profit made by Rupert and in essence a constructive trust over assets of the trust.

On this basis, the Tax Office failed in their attempt to tax the arrangements.

In contrast, Robert Holmes à Court (or the 'briefcase case') is another high profile example.

Holmes à Court started business life as a lawyer and made first takeover while acting as an administrator for a company. He was the first Australian billionaire through ownership of Heytesbury Pty Ltd.

He was known for his ambitious take-over attempts including trying to take-over BHP, Carlton United Breweries and Elders IXL and selling his stake in Bell Group to Alan Bond.

Holmes à Court died suddenly at an early age without a will.

His will had been fully finalised and issued for signing. Holmes à Court carried the unsigned will in his briefcase for around two years before his death. His intestacy left his wife and 4 children with no guidance as to how to run his empire.

His wife Janet initially ran the company.

This allowed the eldest son (Peter) to pursue his own university interests overseas.

Peter didn't agree with how the company was being run, and said in later interviews 'it was one thing to lose your dad, but it was a real bummer to lose the whole family at the same time'.

Peter claimed they sorted out the family dispute over the estate because everyone could go their own way.

As they described it, the settlement negotiations were 'like war with your own family'.

The final outcome, after years of litigation, was what seems to be a permanent split of the family because Peter who had previously sold his share in the family business as part of the settlement, then built up his own business in direct competition with the family business.

Ironically, it is believed that the ultimate settlement of the family litigation largely reflected the terms of the unsigned will. It is likely that in addition to the very significant legal and professional fees incurred, there would have also been large tax and stamp duty costs triggered by the re-arrangement. All these costs would have been arguably avoided if Robert had signed his will.

NO ESTATE PLAN, MEANS YOU HAVE AN ESTATE PLAN

66The conventional view serves to protect us from the painful job of thinking. **99**

— *John Kenneth Galbraith*

Till death do us part

Client Scenario

THE INTRICACIES OF the legal system regularly confound all participants.

Unfortunately, even the simplest of situations can result in strange and totally unintended outcomes.

When wealth is involved, the difficulties are often magnified.

Many times in recent history, beneficiaries have been given tens and even hundreds of millions of dollars in gifts under an estate, but still seek to challenge the will on the basis of 'inadequate provision'.

In one case, a husband, who lost his wife 15 years before his death, asked his son Andy and daughter Karen if either of them would consider caring for him.

Karen volunteered and devoted almost all of her spare time to doing so. In the last eight years of her father's life, she lived in his house and was effectively his full time carer.

Pursuant to the last will, the father allocated what he understood to be virtually his entire wealth as follows:

a   his house and all its contents (approximate value $300,000) to Karen
b   his cash (approximately $18,000) to Andy
c   any other assets to be divided equally between Andy and Karen.

While sorting his possessions, after his death, Karen found a lotto ticket. On redeeming it, she discovered a first prize of $12 million, unclaimed from some months earlier.

The question for the courts was, who should receive the payout?

Three arguments were raised:

a   Karen was entitled to the contents of the house; the lotto ticket formed part of those contents and therefore, she was solely entitled

b   the lotto ticket was, effectively, cash and therefore, Andy was solely entitled

c   the ticket was neither house contents, as normally understood, nor cash, and therefore, the winnings should be split equally between Karen and Andy.

It was generally accepted that, although the father and Andy had a strong, although not deep relationship, the father was forever indebted to Karen because of the sacrifices she had made, and therefore, at the very least, he would have expected her to receive half of the lotto winnings, if not entitled to all of them.

The court's decision?

The lotto ticket was akin to cash. Cash was to be distributed solely to the son, therefore 100% of the lotto proceeds went to Andy.

For anyone who owns assets of any description jointly with another person (whether it be a spouse, family member, friend or business associate), the law has what is, in theory, a very simple rule; in practice, it is anything but.

Jointly owned assets can be owned in one of two ways.

If an asset is owned by 'joint tenants', it is as if each owner actually owns 100% of the asset. For example, if two spouses own their family home as joint tenants and one spouse dies, the other spouse will have notionally been deemed to have already owned 100%. The provisions of the deceased spouse's will are therefore irrelevant.

In contrast, if the jointly owned asset is owned, in equal shares, as 'tenants in common', each spouse has legal rights only in relation to one half of the property. In that scenario, if one spouse was to pass away, the ownership of the remaining 50% depends on the provisions of the deceased spouse's estate plan. Often estate plans provide that the remaining 50% does pass to the surviving spouse, but this need not necessarily be the case.

Some years ago, a young professional couple from Sydney, named Bruce and Lina, learned the hard way the distinction between joint tenants and tenants in common. Having lived together for 10 years, the couple decided to formalise their relationship and marry, before starting a family.

During their 10 years together, Bruce and Lina had accumulated a significant asset portfolio, including a unit in Sydney's Double Bay. Originally, they had lived in the unit, but in recent years, it had become their investment property.

They also owned a house at Wolli Creek, a blue chip share portfolio and two European cars. All of these assets were owned as joint tenants.

In their personal names, they had some, relatively nominal, superannuation entitlements as well as life insurance.

While they were not 'high net wealth' as usually defined, they certainly had accumulated an impressive array of assets and had been financially responsible at every opportunity. They had also ensured that comprehensive estate planning documentation had been put in place over six years before their marriage.

In lieu of wedding presents, Bruce and Lina requested 'mortgage management assistance' – in other words, cash gifts that would be used to reduce the home loan balance on the Wolli Creek property.

Thanks to the significant generosity of Lina's parents, a 6-figure amount was deposited in the couple's joint bank account as they left for the airport on the following Monday morning, en route to Kangaroo Island.

The flight from Sydney to Adelaide was uneventful.

The flight from Adelaide to the island was unsuccessful.

Of the 8 people on the 12-seater plane that Monday afternoon, 7 died instantaneously and the 8th, the pilot, survived, although he would never walk again. He was never able to explain why doctors discovered excessive amounts of the active ingredient of marijuana in his blood system during routine checks not long after he was recovered from the wreckage.

After some weeks working through the emotional issues that arise from burying a child, Lina's parents, as executors of their late daughter and son-in-law's wills, began the practical process of administering the estate.

One of their first discoveries was that, despite what was set out in them, the wills were in fact irrelevant, including the parents' own appointment as executors of the estates.

Each spouse had appointed the other as the executor and sole beneficiary of the estate, and had stipulated that if they failed to survive each other, Lina's parents would be the executors and the estate would be divided equally between the two sets of families. What they did not provide for was what would happen if the couple were to marry, which, of course, they had.

Regardless of who is nominated as a beneficiary, a will is generally automatically revoked by marriage, unless the will expressly provides otherwise. The wills here had no reference to marriage and were therefore, revoked on the Saturday of the wedding.

By the time of the light plane crash on the Monday afternoon, the newly wedded couple effectively had no estate plan.

Where there is no estate planning documentation in place, the government determines how wealth is to be distributed and the key issue, in relation to jointly owned assets, is whether they are owned as joint tenants or tenants in common.

For Bruce and Lina, virtually their entire asset portfolio was owned as joint tenants.

Where a couple have assets owned as joint tenants die in the same incident, the law has a 'tiebreaker' rule that deems the younger of the couple to have in fact survived the accident by 24 hours.

This notional additional day of life provides the pathway for determining who is entitled to all of the jointly owned assets.

In other words, the last joint tenant to die will own 100% of all assets and, therefore, that estate plan regulates the distribution of all wealth.

In this case, Bruce was some 9 months younger than Lina, so the Double Bay unit, share portfolio, Wolli Creek property and two motor vehicles were, for the purposes of the estate administration, solely his. The cash at bank was also solely his, including the significant 6-figure deposit that had been sourced largely from Lina's parents just a couple of days before the plane crash.

As Bruce died without a valid will, the government rules (namely the intestacy provisions) applied and, under these rules, all his wealth passed to his parents.

The relationship between the two sets of parents had always been at best uncomfortable. As the exact legal position in relation to the assets began to unravel, the relationship became positively hostile, as Bruce's parents refused to share any of the wealth with Lina's parents, and would not return the cash gift that they had made, nor the cash gifts from the wedding guests.

The complete disillusionment of Lina's parents and wider family was heightened further when their proposal that the majority of the wealth be donated to a foundation to support parents or families who lose children at a young age was rejected.

As it turned out, the rejection was partly driven by the fact that Bruce's parents, who had been estranged for some years before the accident, were embarking on what became an extremely drawn out and costly divorce settlement.

So, rather than using the combined wealth of their son and daughter-in-law to provide for other families in the time of need, a significant proportion of the wealth went to cover legal fees.

Court Decision

If a person dies without a will, the law says that their assets will be distributed to their family, as determined by a set formula (the 'intestacy' rules). The set formula is different in every Australian jurisdiction. There are a range of issues which will determine which jurisdiction's rules will apply.

The intestacy rules will also apply where a person dies without a valid will in relation to all of their assets. In this regard, it can in fact be possible to die 'partially intestate'. This simply means that there are assets in a person's estate that are not validly dealt with under the will in place at a person's death.

The following summary gives a broad example of the way in which the intestacy rules often work. If a person dies leaving:

(1) their spouse, but no children: their spouse receives everything;

(2) their spouse and children: their spouse receives the first $150,000 and one half of the balance of the estate if there is one child, or one third of the balance if there is more than one child. The deceased's children share the balance between them;

(3) children but no spouse: their children receive a share each, but only if 18 years of age or married;

(4) no spouse or children: the person's parents will share the estate (if both are alive then equally);

(5) no spouse, no children and no parents: their siblings share equally.

A spouse includes a legal and de facto spouse.

The amount received by each person will depend on the value of the estate and whether any other beneficiaries are entitled to the assets of the deceased.

If the person does not have any family members who qualify, then the assets may pass to the government.

It is necessary that someone apply to the court to be appointed as the administrator, to ensure that the person's estate is properly administered. This normally adds time and significant extra costs to the administration of the estate.

If the deceased has young children and a guardian is needed, an application to the court may also have to be made.

It is important to note that a person can in fact be possible to die 'partially intestate'. This simply means that there are assets in a person's estate that are not validly dealt with under the will in place at a person's death.

The intestacy rules are subject to other legal principles, perhaps most starkly demonstrated by the difference between owning something as joint tenants and tenants in common.

Practically, the distinction normally becomes most relevant at times when it is too late to implement a change – for example on death, litigation or relationship breakdowns.

Owning an asset as a joint tenant means the rule of 'survivorship' applies. This is because no owner owns a specific 'share' in the asset, rather all owners own the asset together, and the last surviving owner will own it absolutely.

In contrast where an asset is owned by two or more parties as tenants in common, each party has a discrete defined share in the asset.

This means, if an asset is owned (for example) 99% by one spouse and 1% by the other spouse it must be owned as tenants is common. This strategy is most often implemented where one spouse is 'at risk'

The main reasons that an at-risk spouse would retain a nominal percentage interest can include:

(1)   Protection against spouse or relationship difficulties.

(2)   Protection against the majority owner seeking to encumber the property. In particular, if there is (for example) a gambling issue that arises, no mortgage may be taken out over the property without the consent of the spouse who owns the nominal interest.

(3)   For ease of security arrangements – often a financier will prefer to see the at-risk spouse's name on title documentation, even if their actual ownership interest is nominal.

(4)   Stamp duty savings. This issue is not as relevant as in days gone by because generally there is no longer any substantial

stamp duty benefit, even if both spouses retain an interest in the property.

In relation to stamp duty, it should be noted that in most states there are concessional provisions which apply where one spouse who owns 100% of a family home and transfers 50% (but no more or less) to their spouse, although the stamp duty concession will apply to either a joint tenancy ownership or tenants in common, as long as if it is tenants in common it is in equal shares (ie 50% each).

In an estate planning exercise it is critical to understand all aspects of the way in which property is owned jointly between parties.

One stark example of this, and an area where confusion often arises, relates to land owned registered on title as being owned as joint tenants is a partnership asset. In this instance, the asset it will be deemed in fact to be effectively owned as tenants in common.

If this deeming rule applies then the death of a partner essentially causes the value of their interest to pass under their will, and not by survivorship to the other owners.

The Partnership Acts in most states codify the rules in this regard. These rules generally state that unless the contrary intention appears, property bought with money belonging to the partnership is deemed to have been bought on account of the partnership and is considered partnership property.

The rules in this area were perhaps best explained in the case of Spence v FCT [1967] HCA 32.

In this case it was relevantly held –

'It is … a mistake to say she got it simply by virtue of her joint tenancy. The legal estate devolved in accordance with the joint tenancy.

To that extent the maxim which was mentioned – 'ius accrescendi inter mercatores locum non habet' – does not apply: see Lindley on Partnership, 11th ed. (1951), p. 428.

But it is applicable in equity; partners who hold as joint tenants in law hold beneficially as tenants in common.

That is an old rule.

It is more exactly stated today in terms of the Partnership Acts (the relevant provisions are ss. 30 and 32 in the Western Australian Act) the legal estate devolves according to its nature and tenure but in trust so far as necessary for the persons beneficially interested; and as between partners land which is partnership property is to be treated as personal estate.'

The 'old rule' reference in the quote above comes from cases such as Lake v. Craddock (1732) 3 P Wms 158; 24 ER 1011.

Tenth Principle

IT DEPENDS

> **When all is said and done, more is usually said than done. If you will do today what others won't, you will do tomorrow what others can't.**
>
> — *Keith Cunningham*

Who am I ?

Client Scenario

RIGHTLY OR WRONGLY, as society becomes more and more complex, so too does the legal system.

For many high net wealth individuals, one of the greatest challenges is remaining 'underneath the radar'.

While there are obviously those who appear to revel in the prospect of being profiled in BRW or one of the News Corp paper's Sunday profiles, due to their wealth, there are just as many who despise the attention and will often go to significant lengths to ensure that their identity and asset portfolios remain out of the public eye.

In many cases, the desire to remain low profile is born out of first-hand experiences, or observing friends or business associates who have encountered difficulties almost solely as a result of being pro-filed in the media.

The most obvious and regular difficulty is encountered in the months after a first appearance in a 'rich list'. It is almost guaranteed that a constant stream of investment advisers, financiers, private eq-uity firms and professionals of virtually every description will offer their services or otherwise look to gain access to wealth, often for the 'next big thing'.

More worryingly, for many, is the possibility that, when things go even remotely wrong, various forms of litigation tend to surface more readily when there is a perception that someone is wealthy.

Traditionally in Australia, trusts have been the preferred structure for high net wealth individuals and business owners to protect their wealth and, where relevant, to maintain confidentiality.

In many cases, companies are formed as stand alone solutions or in conjunction with the trust structure.

Depending on the circumstances, however, these structures are not necessarily the panacea. When used without a clear understanding of the objectives, they can often magnify problems that might otherwise have been manageable.

One of the more high profile examples was in the purchase of one of Australia's most expensive homes. For reasons of confidentiality, a shelf company was used as the purchasing entity.

Unfortunately, through fairly basic, publicly available searches of the Australian Securities and Investments Commission, the full details of the business people controlling the company, including their residential address, were discovered.

Countless examples raise the question about what steps can be taken to guard against both the media and litigants who try to identify people with wealth and to discover what that wealth might be.

In mid 2008, as the full extent of the GFC continued to unravel, we had the opportunity to assist a client, named here as Ivy, who had managed to make astronomical returns on financial investments during that period – something that few other clients had managed to do.

Whether by luck or design, Ivy had 'gone short' on a range of financial instruments, which meant that as the markets continued to plummet, her profits continued to soar.

As seems to be the case with so many people who make their money on the financial markets, most of Ivy's profits were diverted into property investments.

While there was nothing to suggest that any of Ivy's activities were in breach of any laws, she had managed to upset a number of fairly influential people with her trading activities, and a number of media outlets became increasingly interested in how the profits were made, and how they were being spent.

Our challenge was to help Ivy achieve complete privacy in relation to the investment of her wealth and also to ensure the wealth was well protected in the case of any litigation, while also making sure that it was invested in as tax effective a manner as legitimately possible.

Had the preferred choice of investment been anything other than real property, satisfying those three objectives would have been relatively simple. A trust structure would have been put in place and its existence would have effectively remained undisclosed, because the requirement to produce a trust deed is not mandatory.

While a trust structure was the preferred vehicle for property investments, the difficulty was that for numerous commercial reasons, the trust would have to be disclosed on the state government land registry records. As soon as disclosure was made, there would be a pathway for both the media and potential litigants not only to discover the people behind the trust, but also the sums paid to acquire the relevant properties.

Ivy had already endured significant media attention because of the astronomic financial returns; any steps that she might take at this point were likely to be closely analysed. The necessary structure, therefore, needed to be kept completely confidential.

There is a good reason why 'trusts' are so named; for them to work as intended, a significant amount of trust needs to be placed in the structure itself and in the actors involved.

Ivy was to gain a deep understanding of the various issues related to trusts.

First, a company was established to act as the controller of the trust.

The company name was randomly selected from the internet; it had absolutely no association with Ivy, her family, or any of the proposed underlying investments.

The directors of the company were two of the partners from the firm who did Ivy's accounting work. The accounting firm had dozens of partners and literally thousands of clients.

There was no public record of Ivy ever having used the accounting firm.

Perhaps more critically, the shareholders of the company were also partners in the accounting firm.

Setting up a company in this way meant that no matter what searches were done, there would be nothing that could link Ivy to the company.

Importantly, Ivy had no legal right in relation to any aspect of the company.

This ownership structure, of itself, would not necessarily have caused the client any concern, except that it became the trustee of a trust which went on to acquire a number of substantial investment properties and two commercial buildings.

Again, the name of the trust was randomly selected from the internet and the name had no association with Ivy or any of the underlying investments.

The company, which was owned and controlled by the partners in the accounting firm, acted as the trustee for the trust, and therefore, had the sole legal right to make decisions and otherwise conduct the activities and investments of the trust.

Traditionally, the names of the people who are intended to benefit from the trust are listed under the trust deed but here, there were no named beneficiaries. This was to maintain complete confidentiality, as the trust deed would be lodged both with external financiers and with the land registry.

External financiers are required by law to maintain complete confidentiality but, in some instances, this confidentiality can be breached.

More relevantly, however, the documents lodged at the land registry can potentially be reviewed by anyone, at any time, on the payment of a nominal fee.

Having lent the funds to the trust to allow it to make the various purchases, Ivy had to rely on the trustee to utilise various powers under the rules of the trust in order to do three things:

a   produce a separate document listing the names of the intended beneficiaries

b   grant Ivy the power to remove the trustee at any time at her absolute discretion

c   appoint Ivy to act as the attorney of the trust in relation to day-to-day activities that did not have any realistic prospect of attracting public attention.

The chances of the accountants acting against Ivy's best interests were probably remote but, given the funds involved, Ivy had placed a significant amount of trust in the accountants. Within a few months of setting up the structure and acquiring the various properties, Ivy was grateful for the lengths to which the trustees had gone in ensuring her three objectives were achieved.

One media outlet had been closely monitoring all the places that she visited and, based on a pattern of visits, started doing property searches based on the street addresses. Having determined that two of the three properties searched were owned by the same company, the journalist gained access to the trust instrument only to discover it was one of the few trusts in Australia that did not list any potential beneficiaries.

While the journalists (and for that matter, any potential litigants) might surmise as to whom the trust was intended to benefit, the level of confidence that they had in the results of their investigative journalism was evidently low.

Ivy has not featured in any of the 'rich list' articles since the structure was put in place, even though, solely on the basis of the two properties that were 'identified', she would have fairly easily satisfied the criteria.

Court Decision

The vagrancies of the estate planning and the application of the 'it depends' principle are almost limitless.

Two interesting examples in areas that are at times overlooked are outlined below.

In the case of MacDowell & Williams and Ors [2012] FamCA 479, the court denied the request for disclosure of the wills and documents relating to the corporate and trust structures of wife's parents.

The wife and the husband married in April 2004 and separated on a final basis on 12 July 2010. The husband had submitted that the documents requested were relevant to the marital property pool and in determining the financial resources available to the wife.

The wife's parents filed an objection to the husband's request on the basis that:

a the documents sought from them in their personal capacity were not relevant as they maintained testamentary capacity; and

b the documents sought from them in their capacity as directors were not relevant as neither the wife nor the husband had any proprietary interest.

In relation to the parents' wills, the court said the request was a 'fishing expedition' by the husband. Although there may be compelling circumstances which warrant the disclosure of will documents (for example, when a parent has lost capacity), here, both parents were alive, in good health and possessed full testamentary capacity.

In relation to the financial and corporate documents, it was held that there was no evidence to suggest that the wife had control over any of the entities, or that control was likely to arise in the future.

The court then considered the previous distributions of one trust where the wife was both the primary and default beneficiary. Given, however, that the wife had only received $28,000 over the ten years of the existence of the trust, and during that time, distributions had also been made to other beneficiaries of the trust, the court held that it was clearly 'discretionary' in nature.

The husband also sought to rely on purported interpretation of Kennon v Spry (profiled elsewhere in this book) and argue that the wife's interests in the trust were property, that being her 'right to consideration' and 'due administration'.

The court held in favour of the wife's parents that this was a misstatement of the law on this point and that while such rights could be taken into account, they would generally be very difficult to value.

The court also bluntly distinguished Spry by noting that Dr Spry had total ultimate control of the trust in question, which was not the case here.

The court did ultimately hold that the wills did not need to be disclosed to the husband on the basis that the parents had full testamentary capacity and may change their wills, or indeed, may otherwise spend or dispose of a substantial part of their wealth.

Interestingly however, the court did specifically note that if the wife's parents had lost capacity or could be shown to be in extremely poor health, then it may have created a situation where the wills would be required to be disclosed.

Another interesting example of the interplay of long standing estate planning rules and the more esoteric concept of 'it depends' is the decision in Dagenmont Pty Ltd v Lugton [2007] QSC 272.

The background in this case was as follows:

(1)   an agreement was entered into by the original appointor of a discretionary trust and other family members in control of the corporate trustee, where, as part of an estate planning exercise, the appointor would resign from various roles in the trust, in return for guaranteed distributions from the trust;

(2)   the distributions were set at an amount of $150,000 each year, indexed for inflation;

(3)   the agreement by the trustee to make these future distributions was effectively a fetter on its future discretion which for centuries has been prohibited;

(4)   each party received independent legal advice at the time of the agreement, however some years later the trustee attempted to cease the distributions due to the, argued, invalid fettering of its discretion.

The court specifically acknowledged the general prohibition on a trustee fettering its discretion, confirming -

> 'trustees cannot fetter the future exercise of powers vested in trustees ... any fetter is of no effect. Trustees need to be properly informed of all relevant matters at the time they come to exercise their relevant power.'

In what is regarded as the first recorded decision allowing a trustee to be bound by an otherwise invalid fettering of its discretion the court confirmed -

a   a provision in a document authorising a trustee to release powers which they would otherwise have a duty to exercise is valid;

b   here the document confirming the agreement between the parties was in essence a release by the trustee of the power conferred on to exercise an unfettered discretion to distribute amongst all potential beneficiaries;

c   alternatively, the agreement effectively amounted to a variation of the terms of the original trust deed;

d   this meant that what would otherwise have been an unfettered trustee discretion became reduced in scope, simultaneously with an obligation being imposed on the trustee (created by the agreement with the original appointor) to distribute the annual amount of $150,000 (indexed);

e   arguably particularly where parties receive independent advice at the time, the court should uphold bargains where it can, rather than destroy them, regardless if the fact that there may be hundreds of years of case law otherwise prohibiting the agreement.

Index

Acknowledgement

This book is the result of contributions from a number of people, each of whom I thank.

In particular:

- The team I work with at View Legal, provide an environment dedicated to continual improvement.

- Our sharing of knowledge as a team is reflected by the sharing of knowledge in our various publications, this book being another example.

- All members inspire me to do better each day, and particular thanks goes to Naomi Arnold, Patrick Ellwood and Tara Lucke for constantly raising our standards.

- Finally, thank you to my family, for being on this journey with me.

Interested to learn more?

View has invested heavily to help advisers help their clients.

Some popular examples of adviser tools are as follows:

1. Subscribe to the free weekly blog posts:

http://blog.viewlegal.com.au/?m=1

To subscribe to the blog, simply enter your email address in the subscription box in the right hand column or alternatively, subscribe through your preferred RSS feed from your browser.

2. View Intellectual Property platform (VIP)

The VIP subscription platform provides you with free access to our webinars, as well as discounted access to our books, entity establishment, superannuation and estate planning solutions.

Even if you trial the VIP platform to update your own estate planning and structuring arrangements it represents fantastic value.

Learn more at—

http://viewlegal.com.au/view-vip-subscription-platform-2/

3. Education programs

View Legal specialises in all forms of adviser education and collaborative learning.

We are fortunate to regularly present to accountants, financial planners, other lawyers and risk advisers.

Our programs are tailored to meet your specific requirements and can be delivered in lengths ranging from 20 minute web-based updates to 5 day in-house courses (and every permutation in between) and formats including in person, webinar and video streaming. Our most popular sessions tend to be 90 minute team trainings, which can be recorded for future use.

A sample of some of our current topics is
set out at the following link —

http://viewlegal.com.au/product-category/events/

Or simply stream or purchase DVD copies of
previous programs via the following link —

http://viewlegal.com.au/recorded-webinars/

A Selection of Other Books from View Legal

For all the latest books please visit
https://viewlegal.com.au/product-category/books/

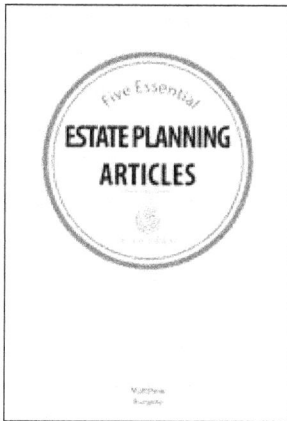

ESTATE PLANNING ARTICLES — Five Essential

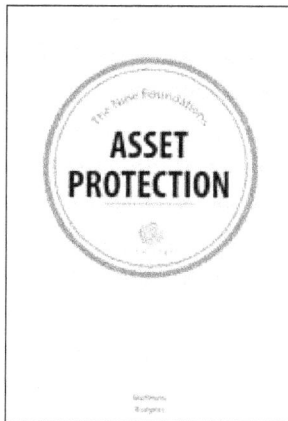

ASSET PROTECTION — The New Foundations

TAXATION OF TRUSTS

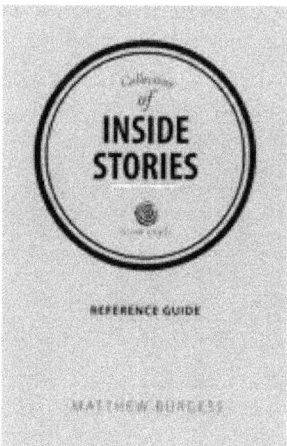

INSIDE STORIES — REFERENCE GUIDE

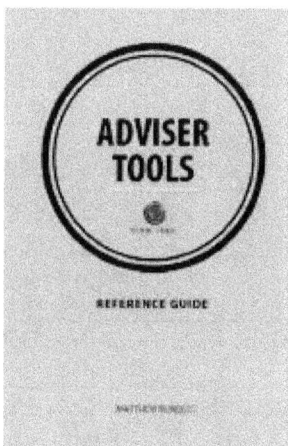

ADVISER TOOLS — REFERENCE GUIDE

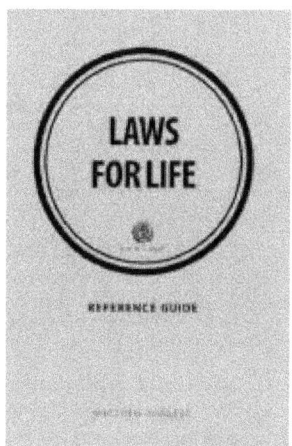

LAWS FOR LIFE — REFERENCE GUIDE

About View

At View Legal our mantra is to be 'for friends'.

In other words creating solutions and value propositions that are compelling to our friends.

To achieve our vision, we have set out to fundamentally and radically revolutionise access to high quality legal advice, in our areas of deep specialisation—structuring, tax, trusts, asset protection, business sales, estate and succession planning.

To help explain the approach View is taking to uniquely deliver valuable legal solutions, the following table lists 10 traditional ways law firms have operated (and, almost exclusively, continue to operate) and the new vision that View is built around.

Old view	View Legal
Bill clients on hourly rates (or various, increasingly elaborate, permutations on the theme) and have no particular interest in client perception of value	Customers provided up front 'SPS Guarantee'— that is service and price satisfaction is guaranteed with all work undertaken following upfront fixed pricing
Everything tracked on a timesheet. The longer something takes, the better	No timesheets. Sophisticated project management tools used to help ensure customer expectations are exceeded
Quality is defined by the law firm	Quality is defined by the customer
'Impressive' CBD office space, with 'dominant' fit outs	View meets where best suits customers. No permanent CBD space retained
Intellectual property is how we make money and should be guarded jealously	Intellectual property is how we create trust and should be shared freely
Lawyers striving to deliver near-perfect technical excellence	All service designed to be fit-for-purpose, aligning with collaboratively agreed customer objectives
Lawyers cultural focus on 'is this billable' for the firm	Lawyers cultural focus on 'is this valuable' for the customer
'Leveraging' of full-time lawyers to do the bulk of the work serving clients	Flexible work practices that match supply with demand
Constant focus on the 'need for diversity' of gender	Only focus on diversity of thought
Revenue growth the #1 goal	Exceeding customer expectations #1 goal

Significant inspiration provided by VeraSage. Partly adapted with permission of George Beaton, Beaton Capital.

If you would like to learn more about any of the above solutions or View more generally contact 1300 View 00 (1300 843 900), email mail@viewlegal.com.au or contact one of the founders listed at the foot of our home page at - http://viewlegal.com.au/

Testimonials

A selection of testimonials for presentations by View (including for organisations such as The Tax Institute, various law societies, Television Education Network, AMP, NAB and ALPMA) are as follows:

Excellent session. Full of interactivity and practical examples/cases.

I wanted to send you a quick note to say that I thought the session you presented was superb and certainly in my top 2 for the entire event.

Your session was the one that we were able to take away the most useful information. We managed to totally can our latest project and built a new one by the time we hit the airport to head home!

Thank you for your excellent presentation at the conference today. In a sentence, it was very inspiring.

Your session was unreal. Very engaging, honest and fun.

Your presentation was simply fantastic! A lesson in how to take the dull and boring and make it fun and entertaining.

About the Author

Matthew Burgess is one of the founders of specialist firm View Legal.

Having the opportunity to help clients achieve their goals is what he is most passionate about.

As Matthew always works in conjunction with trusted advisers (whether it be accountants, financial advisers or other lawyers) and their clients, finding ways to fundamentally improve the value received by those advisers, and in turn their clients, has led him to develop numerous game changing models. Examples include providing guaranteed upfront fixed pricing, founding what is widely regarded as Australia's first virtual law firm, and more recently, developing a platform that gives advisers access to market leading advice and support for less than $1 a week.

Matthew's specialisation in tax, structuring, asset protection, estate and succession planning has seen him recognised by most leading industry associations including the Tax Institute, the Weekly Tax Bulletin and in the 2014 'Best Lawyers' list for trusts and estates and since 2015 in 'Doyles' for taxation.

Work is one aspect of his life Matthew loves, so there is no need to be constantly searching for 'balance'. His other great loves are:

- Family – they are profiled in various ways through the series of children's books he has written under the pseudonym 'Lily Burgess' – see www.wordsfromdaddysmouth.com.au and various TV commercials;

- Learning – going cold Turkey on television and most forms of media in late 2005 has radically increased Matthew's ability

to study the great authors and inspired him to recently publish a book that explores the concept of 'true success' – see www.thedreamenabler.com.au

- Health – aside from being a foodie and swimming at least a 5km a week, Matthew installed a stand up workstation in 2007 and among a few other lifestyle choices, it changed his life.

www.ingramcontent.com/pod-product-compliance
Lightning Source LLC
Chambersburg PA
CBHW061258220326
41599CB00028B/5700